Big Metric Ninja Foodi Cookbook UK

1200-Day Easy & Healthy Air Fry, Pressure Cook, Slow Cook and More Ninja Foodi Recipes Using European Measurement

KYLE COLES

© Copyright 2022 - All rights reserved.

ISBN: ISBN: 9798431234392

The contents of this book may not be reproduced, duplicated or transmitted without direct written permission from the author. Under no circumstances will any legal responsibility or blame be held against the publisher for any reparation, damages, or monetary loss due to the information herein, either directly or indirectly.

Legal Notice:
This book is copyright protected. This is only for personal use. You cannot amend, distribute, sell, use, quote or paraphrase any part of the content within this book without the consent of the author.

Disclaimer Notice:
Please note the information contained within this document is for educational and entertainment purposes only. Every attempt has been made to provide accurate, up to date and reliable information. No warranties of any kind are expressed or implied. Readers acknowledge that the author is not engaging in the rendering of legal, financial, medical or professional advice. The content of this book has been derived from various sources. Please consult a licensed professional before attempting any techniques outlined in this book. By reading this document, the reader agrees that under no circumstances are is the author responsible for any losses, direct or indirect, which are incurred as a result of the use of information contained within this document, including, but not limited to, —errors, omissions, or inaccuracies.

TABLE OF CONTENTS

BREAKFAST RECIPES
Chunky Chips	13
Cottage Pie	14
Loaded omelette	15
Oatmeal	16
Bacon and potato hash	17
Cheesy baked eggs	18
Crispy French toast	19
Kedgeree	20
Cheesy Courgette Muffins	21

FISH & SEA FOOD RECIPES
Salmon Fishcakes	22
Herbed Salmon	23
Teriyaki salmon	24
Prawn pasta	25
Breaded fish goujons	26
Clam chowder	27
Fried shrimp	28
Tuna casserole	29
Fish pie	30
Shrimp boil	31
Shrimp alfredo	32
Easy Fish Pie	33
Smoky Fish Gratin	34
Garlic and Herbs Fish Pie	35

BEEF, LAMB & PORK RECIPES
Roast Lamb with Ginger	36
Roast Lamb with Garlic	37
Lamb and Bean Hotpot	38
Beef Stew with Dumplings	39
Roast beef	40
Sausage and onion gravy	41
Corned beef and cabbage	42
Spring Beef and Vegetable	43
Beef and Root Veg Hotpot	45
Pork Sandwiches with Apple	46
Leek Rarebit Pork Steaks	47
Mushroom and Creamy Mustard Pork Steaks	48
Sweet and Sour Pork	49
Sichuan peppercorn steak	50
Chili verde	51

CHICKEN RECIPES
Chicken and Herb Bake	52
with Tomatoes	52
Spring Roasted Chicken	53
with Tarragon	53
Sticky Chicken Wings	54
Sunday Roast Chicken	55
Chicken taco bowl	56
Chicken fajitas	57
Spatchcock chicken	58
Chicken and mushroom	59
Chicken satay	60

VEGETABLE RECIPES

Stuffed Courgettes with Rocket Salad	61
Raw Kale Tabbouleh with Fried Halloumi	62
Buffalo cauliflower bites	63
Mashed potato	64
Mushroom Risotto	65
Leek and Potato Soup	66
Steamed broccoli	67
Roasted root vegetables	68
Tater Tots	69
Fried cabbage	70
Potato salad	71
Lentil soup	72
Courgette fritti	73
Baked potatoes	74

DESSERT RECIPES

Chocolate mousse	75
Rice Pudding	76
Chocolate Brownies	77
American fluffy pancakes	78
Sesame seed pretzel bites	79
Peach cobbler	80
Berry Oat Crumble Tart	81
Bread and butter pudding	82

CONCLUSION 83
INDEX 84

A Recipe Has No Soul.
You, as the Cook, Must Bring Soul to the Recipe

Thomas Keller

Welcome

Have you ever dreamed of a tool that could replace four or even five kitchen machines? I am sure that you are most likely familiar with the lack of space to put all the appliances in the kitchen and make it comfortable for yourself. a pressure cooker is a unique miracle machine that has many talents. Imagine that now you don't need to buy a slow cooker, pressure cooker, rice cooker, steamer, yogurt machine, or any other useful pots - all these functions already exist in this multitalented device.

The utility of the appliance also means that using the Ninja Foodi, you will be able to craft all of your dishes from mains, desserts to yogurt and even baked goods!
The Ninja Foodi Multi-Crisp Cooker is nothing short of a revolutionary cooking appliance that has seemingly taken the whole culinary world by storm!
Developed by a team of food industry experts and produced by one of the world's most well-known food technology firms, the Ninja Foodi Multi-Crisp Cooker has received numerous awards in it's brief little existence! Of course, these are secondary accolades to the prize of greater culinary adoration offered by this cooking appliance!
As one of the first cooking appliances to be sold on the consumer market that has actually been designed and built to cook. And not just heat! In fact, the Ninja Foodi Multi-Crisp Cooker offers next-level precision, versatility and ingredients haven't been seen in any kitchen up to this point! Helping you to cook food exactly the way you want it!
You know those nice, crispy, golden brown chicken nuggets you get from the fast food joint down the street? You can make those with the Ninja Foodi Multi-Crisp Cooker! No, you're not limited to just deep frying dishes with this appliance either. The Ninja Foodi Multi-Crisp Cooker can also deep fry vegetables and recipe-ready meals!

This is the 21st Century, where dieting has become a big deal in the modern world and a lot of restaurants are getting on board with the idea of incorporating healthier ingredient options into their menu. Especially for kids eat.
To get the perfect food, it's very important to keep the pressure cooker clean. Wash the kitchen tool thoroughly after each use. Cleaning the pressure cooker does not take much time and effort. To do this, you need a cloth or fabric and a dishwasher and vinegar. The heat that the dishwasher gets rid of any fat residue in the pot while vinegar eliminates the smell that remains after cooking.
It is worth remembering that you need to wash only the removable parts of the device. Also, you should unplug the pressure cooker before extracting parts from the gadget.
Make sure that all the washed parts of the pressure cooker are completely dry before placing them back into the pressure cooker. Another easy way to clean the pressure cooker by hand is to combine the vinegar, water, and 1 tablespoon of lemon juice in the pressure cooker and set the program to "Steam. " This method will clean the pot without using a dishwasher or doing so by hand and help you to avoid the smell after cooking pressure cooker.

You will get easy to make recipes, meat, poultry, seafood, the list goes on!
And if you are daring and want to take on more of a challenge, then a good number of slightly complicated recipes are also there to challenge your inner chef!
All of these recipes are carefully chosen to help you lose weight in the long run and become a "Better" version of yourself!

Essentials of Ninja Foodi Pressure Cooker and Air Fryer

1. What's the Ninja Foodi

The Ninja Foodie is probably the most versatile, and undoubtedly revolutionary kitchen appliance out there in the market.

This is the only appliance of its kind that can work as Slow Cooker, Saute pan, Electric Pressure Cooker, Rice Cooker, and even an Air Fryer! All under one hood.

The unique technology that allows its designers to blend the functionalities of Air Fryer and Pressure Cooker means that chefs can cook their food more efficiently and faster than any other kitchen appliance to date.

And just in case you are wondering, with this amazing device, you won't only be limited to simple pressure cooker dishes! The versatility of this appliance will allow you to create anything from soups, stews, chili's to breakfast and desserts! Your imagination is the only limitation here.

For new beginners though, the barrage of functionalities might seem a little bit confusing at first, but rest assured, the appliance is very easy to use.

All you need is a little understanding of what each function button does, and you are good to go!

2. Ninja Foodi VS. Instant Pot/Slow Cooker/Air Fryer

At its heart, the core difference between all three of the above-mentioned appliances and the Ninja Foodi is that the Ninja Foodi is the combination of all three. Meaning, with this revolutionary appliance, you will be able to Pressure Cook, Slow Cook, and even Air Fryer your meals with ease.

Asides from that, there are some fundamental differences that you should about as well.

Considering the Ninja Foodi and Air Fryer:
The Air Fryer is essentially an appliance that is strictly designed for just the purpose of Air frying various and preparing various meals, using the minimum amount of oil. This appliance is excellent at what it does and using an Air Fryer; you can prepare a plethora of different types of meals. However, it is not an all in one.

Comparing the Ninja Foodi with an Air Fryer, you would immediately notice that they both sport a very distinctive shape. The Ninja Foodi is like a round pot, similar to the Instant Pot while the Air Fryer extrudes a little a bit on the top side.

The Crisping Lid alongside the TenderCrisp technology that allows the Ninja Foodi to Air Fry meals, while working as an advanced and versatile is what sets it apart from the Air Fryer.

Considering the Ninja Foodi and Instant Pot and Slow Cooker: The Slow Cooker and Instant Pot are probably the two appliances can be considered as being the closest sibling to the Ninja Foodi Electric Pressure cooker!

All three of the appliances sport a similar shape, which is like a pot.

However, general Slow Cookers are only designed to do just one thing that is to cook your meals for an extended period at extremely low temperatures. (There are multifunctional Slow Cookers, but we are not considering them here).

Instant Pots, on the other hand, are multifunctional Electric Pressure Cookers, which were pretty much the king of the game until the arrival of the Ninja Foodi, which might dethrone them. Similar to the Ninja Foodi, Instant Pot's also come packed with a large number of different features that allows users to bake, roast, simmer, boil, steam and pressure cook their meals.

However, the crucial point where the Ninja Foodi stands out is that alongside most of the features of the Instant Pot and Slow Cooker, the Ninja Foodi is capable of Air Frying meals using the Crisping Lid and TenderCrisp technology.

So in short, the Ninja Foodi is essentially the combination of all three appliances in on nifty package.

3. Uncover Secret of the Revolutionary Tendercrisp Technology

The Tendercrisp Technology stands at the heart of the Ninja Foodi cooking appliance that seemingly differentiates itself from the rest of the world. So, I strongly believe that it is really important that you have a good understanding of what this unique technology does.

So when you are pressure cooking tough ingredients such as meats, you end up with meals that are extremely juicy and satisfying to eat, but tender as well. Just pressure cooking alone won't be able to provide you with any crispy finish! This is where Air Frying comes in.

Air Frying utilizes the power of air to make foods crispier by giving it a nice tasty crust.

The revolutionary technology used in the Ninja Foodi allows a user to infuse both the effects of Pressure Cooking and Air Frying using just the single device! This basic cooking principle of combining both cooking methods is known as Ninja Foodi's proprietary TenderCrisp Technology.

In short, it allows you to create meals that are extremely tender and juicy on the side while having a satisfying crust on the surface.

The basic cooking procedure will ask you first to cook you a meal using pressure cooking, then use the Crisping Lid and Crisping Basket accompanied by the Air Crisp function to achieve your desired level of crispiness.

To better understand the mechanism at work here, the TenderCrisp technology utilizes superheated steam to infuse both flavors and moisture into your pressure cooked food.

Afterward, the crisping lid blows extremely hot air to every side of your meal that gives it a fine golden color and crisp finish.

This unique combination is so far unachievable by any other appliance to date!

4. Different Function Buttons of the Ninja Foodi

Given the versatility of the Ninja Foodi, it is very easy to understand why some individuals might get confused when dealing with the plethora of amazing functions available in the appliance.

To make things easier for you and ensure that you don't have to face any troubles in the future, I have tried to outline the basic functions of all of the buttons present in most models of the Ninja Foodi.

PRESSURE COOKER

Let's first talk about the single feature that you will be using most of the time. The Pressure function will allow you to use your Ninja Foodi as a Pressure Cooker appliance and cook your meals as you would in an electric pressure cooker such as the Instant Pot.

In this feature, foods are cooked at high temperature under pressure.

Just make sure to be careful when releasing the pressure! Otherwise, you might harm yourself.

There are essentially two ways through which you can release the pressure, which is discussed later on in the chapter.

STEAM

Asides from Air Crisp, the Steam Function is probably one of the healthiest cooking option available in the Foodi!

The basic principle is as follows- Water is boiled inside the Ninja Foodi that generates a good amount of steam. This hot steam is then used to cook your ingredients kept in a steaming rack situated at the top of the inner chamber of your Pot.

Steaming is perfect for vegetables and other tender foods as it allows to preserve the nutrients while maintaining a nice crispy perfectly.

Asides from vegetables, however, the Steam function can also be used for cooking various fish and seafood, which are much more delicate than other red meats and chicken.

The process of steaming fish are the same, all you have to do is place them on the steaming rack.

Steaming the fish helps to preserve the flavor and moisture as well perfectly.

SLOW COOKER

Despite popular belief, some foods tend to taste a whole lot better when Slowly Cooked over extremely low temperature for hours on end. This is why Slow Cookers such as the CrockPot are so popular amongst chefs and house makers!

The Slow Cooker feature of the Ninja Foodi allows you to achieve the same result, but without the need for a different appliance.

Ideal scenarios to use the Slow Cooker function would be when you want to cook your foods for longer to bring out the intense flavor of spices and herbs in stews, soups, and casseroles.

Since it takes a lot of time to Slow Cook, you should prepare and toss the ingredients early on before your feeding time.

For example. If you want to have your Slow Cooker meal for breakfast, prepare ingredients the night before and add them to your Foodi. The Foodi will do its magic and have the meal prepared by morning.

The Slow Cooker feature also comes with a HIGH or LOW setting that allows you to decide how long you want your meal to simmer.

START/STOP BUTTON

The function of this particular button is pretty straightforward; it allows you to initiate or stop the cooking process.

SEAR/SAUTE

The Browning/Saute or Sear/Saute mode of the Ninja Foodi provides you with the means to brown your meat before cooking it using a just a little bit of oil. This is similar to when you are browning meat on a stovetop frying pan. And keeping that in mind, the Ninja Foodie's browning mode comes with five different Stove Top temperature settings that allow you to set your desired settings with ease.

Asides from browning meat, the different Stove Top temperatures also allows you to gently simmer your foods, cook or even sear them at very high temperatures.

Searing is yet another way to infuse the delicious flavors of your meat inside and give an extremely satisfying result.

This particular model is also excellent if you are in the mode for a quick Sautéed vegetable snack to go along with your main course.

AIR CRISP

This is probably the feature that makes the Ninja Foodi so revolutionary and awesome to use! The Tendercrisp lid that comes as a part of the Ninja Foodi allows you to use the appliance as the perfect Air Fryer device.

Using the Tendercrisp lid and Air Crisp mode, the appliance will let you bake, roast, broil meals to perfection using just the power of superheated air! In the end, you will get perfectly caramelized, heartwarming dishes.

The Foodi comes with a dedicated crisping basket that is specifically designed for this purpose, which optimizes the way meals are air fried in the Foodi.

But the best part in all of these is probably the fact that the using the Air Crisp feature, you will be able to cook your meals using almost none to minimal amount of oil!

It is also possible to combine both the pressure cooking mechanism and Air Crisp function to create unique and flavorful dishes.

The Pressure cooking phase will help you to seal the delicious juices of the meal inside the meat, while the crisping lid and Air Crisp mechanism will provide you to cook/roast your meal to perfection, giving a nice heartfelt crispy finish.

This combined method is also amazing when roasting whole chicken meat or roasts, as all the moisture remains intact and the final result turns out to be a dramatic crispy finish.

BAKE/ROAST

For anyone who loves to bake, this function is a dream come true! The Bake/Roast function allows the Foodi to be used as a traditional convection oven. This means you will be do anything that you might do with a general everyday oven! If you are in the mode to bake amazing cakes or casseroles, the Foodi has got you covered!

Broil

The main purpose of the Broil function is to allow you to use your appliance like an oven broiler and slightly brown the top of your dish if required. If you are in the mood for roasting a fine piece of pork loin to perfection or broiling your dish until the cheese melts and oozes, this mode is the perfect one to go with!

DEHYDRATE

In some more premium models of the Ninja Foodi appliance, you will notice a function labeled as "Dehydrate." This particular function is best suited for simple dried snacks such as dried apple slices, banana chips, jerky, etc. As you can probably guess, the core idea of this function is to suck out the moisture and dehydrate your ingredient into a hearty edible snack.

5. The Different Parts and Accessories of the Ninja Foodi

The different parts of the Ninja Foodi are as follows:

- **Pressure Release Valve:** These valves are used to control the entrapment or release of the pressure inside the pot.
- **Pressure Lid:** The pressure lid is used when pressure is cooking your meals.
- **Crisping Lid:** The crisping lid is used when trying to Air Fryer your meals using the TenderCrisp technology.
- **Cooking Pot:** The cooking pot is the actual inner pot where you dump the ingredients and let it cook.

Asides from the above-mentioned core parts, there are some others that you should know about as well.

The Reversible Rack: This particular rack can be used both ways for your desired effect. The reversible rack is primarily used for broiling (when placed in the upper position), while it can also be used for steaming, cooking, baking, and roasting, should you choose to place it in the lower position.

Cook and Crisp Basket: The crisping basket is an easily removable basket that is specially designed for Air Crisping.

Various other accessories are also available for the Ninja Foodi. Some of the more useful ones are as follows:

Extra Reversible Rack/ 8 Inch Round Wire Cooling Rack: Some recipes might ask you to use a rack twice, once for steaming and once for broiling for example. Instead of using the same rack over and over again, it's a pretty good idea to have an extra rack around, and it makes life a whole lot easier.

And as a bonus, you will also be able to use it as a cooling rack as well.

Extra Sealing Ring: Overtime and despite your best efforts, the Silicone ring might pick up dirt and unpleasant odor. Despite its pretty long-lasting durability, they tend to become nicked or stretched after prolonged usage!

Having a damaged or compromised Sealing Ring is never a good idea as it will render your pot useless in the future. Therefore, keeping an extra ring always helps in the long run. You when buying an extra ring, make sure to check that you are buying a ring that is specifically designed for the Foodi. Otherwise, it won't fit properly.

Multi-Purpose Pan/Metal/Ceramic Bowl: If you do a lot of Pot-In-Pot cooking, then having a ceramic or metal bowl would be a Godsend! These are excellent for when you are making dishes such as quiches, casseroles or even cake. Just make sure to buy a one that it no more than about 8 and ½ inches across. The official Multi-Purpose Pan sold by Ninja is excellent for this purpose.

Roasting Rack Insert: This rack is specifically designed to work with the Cook and Crisp Basket, and comes in real handy if you want to roast or glaze meat/ribs.

Cook and Crisp Layered Insert: This layout helps to increase the capacity of the Cook and Crisp Basket by allowing you to create layers of meals and crisp them all at once.

6. Amazing advantages of the Ninja Foodi

At its heart, the Ninja Foodi is an electric pressure cooker, and making foods utilizing this single aspect will yield you extremely juicy and tender meals in no time!

But why should you limit yourself to only that?

Asides from being able to prepare mouthwatering pressure cooked and fried air meals, the Ninja Foodi comes with a plethora of advantages that will make your cooking experience even more delightful.

Below are just some of the many!

Allows you to cook frozen food: With the awesome power of the Ninja Foodi, you will be able to save a huge amount of time by skipping the "defrosting" phase and adding your meat right out of the freezer! The advanced cooking technologies allow the Foodi to defrost the meat and cook them to perfection in no time!

Let's you cook healthier meals: The precise cooking mechanism of the Ninja Foodi allows the appliance to preserve most of the nutrition of your meal while ensuring that your meals are undeniably delicious.

Acts as a one-stop shop: This single appliance acts as a one-stop shop for all of your meals! You can cook, roast, steam in the single pot itself and have everything ready by the end!

Allows cooking in a single pot: Just using a single pot, you will be able to convert a simple and regular looking soup into an amazing casserole dish or something exquisite. The versatility of the Ninja Foodi means that you won't have to use multiple pots for your cooking, the single pot provided with the Foodi is more than enough to prepare your meal from scratch to finish.

Frees up a lot of kitchen space: Regardless the size of your kitchen, the ergonomic design of the Ninja Foodi means that you will always be able to make up space for this nifty appliance! And since this pot can perform the job of a Slow Cooker, Air Fryer, Pressure Cooker, etc. all alone, you won't even have to keep any other appliances around!

Easy Cleaning: Cleaning is a nightmare for every chef and homemaker! Since all the cooking is done in a ceramic coated non-stick pot in the Ninja Foodi, cleaning the appliance is a breeze! All it takes is a little bit of soapy water, and you are good to go!

Kills Any And All Harmful Micro-Organism: Sophisticated Electric Pressure Cookers such as the Ninja Foodi allows the internal temperature inside the pot to reach extremely high levels! This allows the pot to destroy most viruses and bacteria that might otherwise be harmful to your body. Some of the more resistant ones found in raw maize or corns can also be destroyed as well.

7. Useful Tips for Ninja Foodi Cooking

As time goes on, you will learn how to utilize the power of your Ninja Foodi to its full extent.

However, the following tips will help you during the early days of your life with the Foodi and ensure that your experience is as pleasant and smooth as possible.

- It is crucial that you don't just press the function buttons randomly! Try to read through the function of each button and use them according to the requirement of your recipe.
- This is something that many people don't know, once the cooking timer of your appliance hits '0', the pot will automatically go into "Natural Pressure Release" mode where it will start to release the pressure on its own. You can use a quick release anytime to release all the steam at once, or you can wait for 10-15 minutes until the steam vents off.
- It is important that you place the lid properly while closing the appliance as it greatly affects the cooking. Therefore, make sure that your lid is tightly close by ensuring that the silicone ring inside the lid is placed all the way around the groove.
- If you are in a rush and want to release the pressure quickly, turn the pressure valve to "Open Position," which will quick release all the pressure. But this can be a little risky as a lot of steam comes out at once, so be sure to stay careful.
- Once your start using the appliance for cooking, make sure to check if the Pressure Valve is in the "Locked Position." If it is not, your appliance won't be able to build up pressure inside for cooking.
- If you are dealing with a recipe that calls for unfrozen meat, make sure to use the same amount of cooking time and liquid that you would use if you were to use frozen meat of the same type.

- Make sure to keep in mind that the "Timer" button isn't a button to set time! Rather it acts as a Delay Timer. Using this button, you will be able to set a specific time, after which the Ninja Foodi will automatically wake up and start cooking the food.

8. Frequently Asked Questions

Below are the answers to some of the most commonly asked questions that should help you clear up some confusion (if you have any).

Why do some foods such as rice, or veggies call for different cooking times in different recipes?

The cooking time does not only depend on the type of ingredient that you are using but on various other factors as well.

When considering vegetables, you have to consider how the veggies are cut. If using a whole cauliflower head, it might be cubed, cut into florets, alternatively, you can have cubed potatoes and whole potatoes.

Cubed variations will always take less time than the whole veggie itself.

The same goes for meat as well, the thickness and the cut largely vary the time taken to cooking the meal properly.

If you are cooking rice, you might be interested to know that pressure cooking rice directly into the pot will cook much faster than pressure cooking the rice in a bowl that is set on the rack.

Is it possible to adjust the temperature of Sautéing or Searing?

Yes, all you have to do is press the Temperature Up and Down arrows twice, and the appliance will change the heat setting and allow you to Saute/Sear at your selected mode.

Is Pre-heating necessary when using the Crisping or Roasting feature?

It is not necessary that you preheat your pot, if you do, you will get better results. Just let the appliance pre-heat for 5 minutes before cooking.

Is it possible to open the lid while cooking?

As long as you are using any of the convection methods such as Air Crisp, Bake/Roast, you are allowed to open the lid at any time you want. Once you open up the lid, the cooking will pause and will only resume once you have securely placed the lid.

However, while Pressure Cooking/Steaming, you should never open the lid until the whole cook cycle and pressure release cycle is complete!

Are the different parts of the Foodi Dishwasher safe?

Yes, all the accessories of the Ninja Foodi are dishwasher safe, alongside the inner pot as well. However, keep in mind that the base, Crisping Lid, and Pressure Lid are NOT dishwasher safe and should be cleaned by using a sponge or wet cloth.

How to get rid of the unpleasant smell from the Sealing Ring?

The most basic step to do is to remove the sealing ring after every cook session and washing/drying I before putting it back. You can do this either by hand or by using your dishwasher. If that doesn't do the trick, try to leave it under the sun for a while.

CHUNKY CHIPS

PREPARATION TIME 10 MINUTES

COOKING TIME 25 MINUTES

SERVINGS 4 PERSONS

INGREDIENTS:
- 250ml water
- 1kg Maris Piper potatoes
- 3 tbsp vegetable oil
- salt, to taste

PREPARATIONS:

1. Place the air fryer basket into the Ninja Foodi pot and add 250ml water.
2. Peel the skin from the potatoes then slice into chunky chips approximately 1cm wide and 7cm long.
3. Place the chunky chips into the Ninja Foodi pot then cover with the lid and turn the back valve to seal. Set to pressure cook on high for 2 minutes then quick-release pressure.
4. Tip the chunky chips into a bowl then drain the water from the inner pot of the Foodi and wipe dry.
5. Drizzle the vegetable bowl over the chunky chips and return to the air fryer basket.
6. Place the lid on the Ninja Foodi and seal, set to air crisp at 220C for 10 minutes.
7. After 10 minutes, remove the lid and gently toss the chips to ensure even cooking.
8. Reseal and set to air crisp at 220C for a further 10 minutes.
9. Once the chunky chips are crisp and golden brown transfer to a plate, season with salt and serve.

CHUNKY CHIPS | BREAKFAST RECIPES

COTTAGE PIE

PREPARATION TIME 20 MINUTES

COOKING TIME 40 MINUTES

SERVINGS 4 PERSONS

INGREDIENTS:

- 1.5kg potatoes, peeled and roughly chopped
- 200g unsalted butter, room temperature
- 100ml milk
- 1 tbsp vegetable oil
- 1 onion, finely chopped
- 1 carrot, finely chopped
- 1 stalk celery, finely chopped
- 2 cloves garlic, finely chopped
- 500g minced beef
- 500ml beef stock
- ½ tsp thyme
- 1 bay leaf
- 1 tbsp Worcestershire sauce
- 100g peas
- salt, to taste

PREPARATIONS:

1. Fill the inner pot of the Ninja Foodi halfway with water then add the chopped potatoes, set to pressure cook for 5 minutes.
2. Quick release the potatoes then strain off the water from the pot.
3. Crush the potatoes using a potato masher then add in butter and milk, continue to mash until the mixture is smooth and thick.
4. Transfer the mashed potato to a dish and season with salt to taste, set aside.
5. Clean out the inner pot of the Ninja Foodi then set to saute on high heat and add the vegetable oil.
6. Stir in the onion, carrot, celery, garlic and minced beef, cook for 5 minutes.
7. Pour the beef stock, thyme and bay leaf into the pot then attach the lid and set to pressure cook on high for 5 minutes.
8. Allow the pot to naturally release then mix in the Worcestershire sauce and peas, season with salt to taste.
9. Spread a layer of mashed potato over the cottage pie base then set the Ninja Foodi to grill at 180C for 10 minutes until a golden crust has formed.

14 | BREAKFAST RECIPES | COTTAGE PIE

LOADED OMELETTE

PREPARATION TIME 10 MINUTES

COOKING TIME 10 MINUTES

SERVINGS 4 PERSONS

INGREDIENTS:

- 1 tbsp unsalted butter
- 1 onion, finely chopped
- 75g sausage, sliced
- 1 tsp garlic powder
- 100g mushroom, thinly sliced
- 8 eggs, lightly beaten
- 100ml single cream
- 75g cheddar cheese, grated
- 2 tbsp chives, finely chopped

PREPARATIONS:

1. Set the Ninja Foodi to SAUTE and add the butter.
2. Stir in the onion and sliced sausage, cook for 5 minutes.
3. Then add the garlic powder and mushrooms, cook for 2 minutes then turn off the Ninja Foodi.
4. In a bowl whisk together the eggs, single cream and cheddar cheese.
5. Pour the egg mixture into the pot then cover with the lid.
6. Set the Ninja Foodi to Air Crisp at 200C for 8 minutes.
7. Tip the loaded omelette out onto a chopping board then fold over to seal.
8. Garnish the omelette with extra cheese and chives.

OATMEAL

PREPARATION TIME 5 MINUTES

COOKING TIME 5 MINUTES

SERVINGS 4 PERSONS

INGREDIENTS:

- 50g unsalted butter
- 500ml water
- 1 red apple, diced
- 50g raisins
- 25g brown sugar
- 80g rolled oats
- ½ tsp ground cinnamon
- 2 tbsp honey

PREPARATIONS:

1. Set the Ninja Foodi to SAUTE then add the butter.
2. Once the butter has melted, turn off the pot then add the water, apple, raisins, brown sugar, oats and ground cinnamon.
3. Place the lid on the Ninja Foodi and set it to COOK on high pressure for 5 minutes.
4. Release the pressure from the pot then stir the honey into the oatmeal.
5. Adjust the consistency of the oatmeal with water or milk then serve.

BACON AND POTATO HASH

PREPARATION TIME
10 MINUTES

COOKING TIME
25 MINUTES

SERVINGS
4 PERSONS

INGREDIENTS:
- 1 tsp olive oil
- 250g bacon, diced
- 1 onion, grated
- 2 baking potatoes, grated
- 2 tbsp plain flour
- 1 tsp smoked paprika
- 1 tsp garlic powder
- 1 tsp fine salt
- 1 tsp black pepper

PREPARATIONS:

1. Program the Ninja Foodi to SAUTE then add the olive oil.
2. Stir the bacon and onion into the pot, cook for 5 minutes.
3. Then add the grated potato, plain flour, smoked paprika, garlic powder, salt and black pepper.
4. Press the bacon and potato hash into an even later then place the lid onto the pot.
5. Set the Ninja Foodi to ROAST at 150C for 20 minutes.
6. Tip the bacon and potato hash onto a serving plate and serve with your favourite eggs.

CHEESY BAKED EGGS

PREPARATION TIME 5 MINUTES

COOKING TIME 10 MINUTES

SERVINGS 4 PERSONS

INGREDIENTS:
- 1 tsp spray oil
- 4 eggs
- 50ml single cream
- 50g spinach
- ¼ tsp fine salt
- ¼ tsp black pepper
- 50g cheddar cheese, grated

PREPARATIONS:
1. Grease the ramekins with spray oil.
2. Into a mixing bowl whisk together the eggs, single cream, spinach, salt and black pepper.
3. Pour the egg mixture evenly into the four ramekins.
4. Top each ramekin with grated cheddar cheese.
5. Place the four ramekins into the Ninja Foodi basket then cover with the lid.
6. Set the pot to 165C for 10 minutes.
7. Allow for a quick release of pressure then serve the cheesy baked eggs.

CRISPY FRENCH TOAST

PREPARATION TIME
5 MINUTES

COOKING TIME
10 MINUTES

SERVINGS
4 PERSONS

INGREDIENTS:

- 250ml single cream
- 1 egg, lightly whisked
- 50g icing sugar
- 1 tsp ground cinnamon
- 4 slices thick white bread
- 2 tbsp honey

PREPARATIONS:

1. Preheat the Ninja Foodi to 180C then add the white bread, toast for 3 minutes.
2. In a bowl whisk together the single cream, egg, icing sugar and ground cinnamon.
3. Dip the toast into the cream mixture then lay into the Ninja Foodi basket.
4. Place the lid onto the pot and set to COOK for 5 minutes until crisp and golden.
5. Serve the crispy French toast with a drizzle of honey.

KEDGEREE

PREPARATION TIME 20 MINUTES

COOKING TIME 40 MINUTES

SERVINGS 4 PERSONS

INGREDIENTS:

- 1 tbsp cooking oil
- 1 onion, chopped
- 2-cm piece ginger, peeled and grated
- 1 garlic clove, crushed
- ½ tsp ground coriander
- ½ tsp ground turmeric
- 1 tbsp medium curry powder
- 250g long grain rice
- 200 mL vegetable stock
- 4 eggs
- 2 tbsp roughly chopped fresh parsley
- 150ml milk
- 400g smoked haddock fillets

PREPARATIONS:

1. For the rice and eggs, add one tablespoon of cooking oil into the inner pot and set settings to SEAR/SAUTÉ. Adjust temperature to "2 inch / 5 cm.
2. Add the onion, ginger, garlic, coriander, turmeric and curry powder and cook for 5 minutes, stirring frequently.
3. Add the rice and stir. Add one cup of vegetable stock and place the Deluxe Reversible Rack over the rice. Place the eggs on the rack. Select the setting to STEAM.
4. Adjust the Pressure Cooker lid and adjust the Air Outlet Vent to VENT.
5. Use the TEMP button and main centre button to set the temperature on high and the TIME setting to set the time to 2 minutes. Press START/STOP, allow the steam to build up, and the timer will start the countdown. Make sure you have the KEEP WARM setting on.
6. Once the two minutes have passed, allow the rice to rest for ten minutes. Remove the eggs and place them on an ice bath. Once cooled down, peel and dice. Scoop out the rice into a mixing bowl.
7. For the fish, rinse the inner pot, dry with paper towels and place it in the Ninja Foodi Pressure Cooker Air Fryer.
8. Add the milk and 100ml of water. Place the fish, skin-side down, adjust the setting to SEAR/SAUTÉ temperature "2 inch / 5 cm and simmer for 5 minutes.
9. Remove the inner pot, drain the fish and flake with a fork. Combine the rice, fish, and hard-boiled eggs cut into quarters. Garnish with parsley.

CHEESY COURGETTE MUFFINS

PREPARATION TIME 15 MINUTES

COOKING TIME 30 MINUTES

SERVINGS 9 PERSONS

INGREDIENTS:
- 1 small courgette
- 100g light cheddar cheese
- 225g self-rising flour
- 50ml olive oil
- 175ml semi-skimmed milk
- 1 egg
- black pepper

PREPARATIONS:

1. Rinse the courgette, cut its ends off and grate. Grate the cheese.
2. In a mixing bowl, combine the grated courgette with the grated Cheddar, self-rising flour, olive oil, milk, egg and black pepper.
3. Transfer the batter into a round silicone cupcake mould lined with cupcake liners. Make sure the mould fits the Ninja Foodi Pressure Cooker Air Fryer.
4. To bake, place the inner pot into the Ninja Foodi Pressure Cooker Air Fryer and the mould over the Deluxe Reversible Rack.
5. Set on PRESSURE cooking, High setting for 13 minutes.
6. Make sure the valve is in the SEAL position.
7. Press START/STOP . Allow the pressure to rise, and the timer will start the countdown.
8. Once the time has passed, release the pressure carefully with the Quick Release valve.
9. Remove the Pressure Cooker lid and the inner pot.
10. To air fry, adjust the setting to AIRFRY at 390°F (200°C) and adjust the timing to 8 minutes. Press START/STOP.
11. Open the lid halfway through and place the Deluxe Reversible Rack with the silicone mould inside the Ninja Foodi Pressure Cooker Air Fryer.
12. Air-fry for the remaining 4 minutes.
13. Safely remove the silicone mould and unmould the courgette muffins.

SALMON FISHCAKES

PREPARATION TIME 15 MINUTES   **COOKING TIME** 45 MINUTES   **SERVINGS** 4 PERSONS

INGREDIENTS:

- 200ml milk
- 300g salmon, skinless and pin-boned
- 700g potato, peeled and roughly chopped
- 200g peas
- 1 lemon, zested and juiced
- 150g breadcrumbs
- 3 tbsp vegetable oil
- salt, to taste

PREPARATIONS:

1. Set the Ninja Foodi to saute on medium heat then add the milk, 200ml water and the salmon, once simmering, cook for 5 minutes.
2. Turn off the pot and allow the fish to poach for 10 minutes in the milk, then remove the fish and place into a bowl, gently flake.
3. Wipe out the inner pot of the Ninja Foodi and fill with water, set to saute on high heat and add the potatoes.
4. Cook the potatoes for 10 minutes until soft then strain off the water.
5. Return the potatoes to the pot along with the peas, use a potato masher to crush.
6. Transfer the mashed potato and peas into the bowl of cooked salmon then add the lemon zest, lemon juice and salt.
7. Shape the salmon mixture into 8 equally sized fishcakes.
8. Fill a bowl with breadcrumbs then coat each salmon fishcake in breadcrumbs to cover.
9. Drizzle the fishcakes with vegetable oil then place the fryer basket into the Ninja Foodi.
10. Seal the lid and set to air fry on 170C for 10 minutes.
11. After 10 minutes, flip the fishcakes and cook for a further 10 minutes.
12. Serve the salmon fishcakes hot with a mayonnaise, tartare sauce or fresh lemon juice.

HERBED SALMON

PREPARATION TIME 10 MINUTES

COOKING TIME 5 MINUTES

SERVINGS 4 PERSONS

INGREDIENTS:

- 4 salmon fillets (approximately 115g each)
- 50g unsalted butter, melted
- 150g panko breadcrumb
- 2 tbsp dill, finely chopped
- 2 tbsp parsley, finely chopped
- 2 tsp Herb de Provence
- 1 tsp garlic powder
- ½ tsp salt
- ½ tsp black pepper

PREPARATIONS:

1. In a bowl stir together the panko breadcrumb, dill, parsley, Herb de Provence, garlic powder, salt and black pepper.
2. Place the salmon fillets skin-side-down into the basket of the Ninja Foodi.
3. Brush the flesh of the salmon with melted butter then top each fillet with the breadcrumb mixture.
4. Place the lid on the Ninja Foodi and set it to COOK for 5 minutes.
5. Allow for a slow release to reveal perfectly cooked fish with a crisp herb crust.

TERIYAKI SALMON

PREPARATION TIME 20 MINUTES

COOKING TIME 10 MINUTES

SERVINGS 4 PERSONS

INGREDIENTS:
- 4 x 125g salmon fillets
- 50ml soy sauce
- 2 tbsp mirin
- 1 tbsp brown sugar
- 2 tsp cornflour
- 1 tsp ginger, grated
- 1 tsp garlic, grated
- 1 tsp sesame oil
- 1 tbsp sesame seeds

PREPARATIONS:

1. Place a saucepan on low heat then add the soy sauce, mirin, brown sugar, cornflour, ginger, garlic and sesame oil.
2. Whisk together the ingredients then bring to a simmer for 2 minutes to thicken.
3. Remove the teriyaki sauce from the heat and allow it to cool.
4. Place the salmon fillets onto a plate then pour over the teriyaki sauce, allow the fish to marinade for 15 minutes.
5. Line the Ninja Foodi basket with parchment paper then lay the salmon fillets into the basket skin-side-down.
6. Set the COOK at 200C and place the basket inside for 10 minutes.
7. Release the pressure from the Ninja Foodi then serve the teriyaki salmon topped with sesame seeds.

PRAWN PASTA

PREPARATION TIME
5 MINUTES

COOKING TIME
15 MINUTES

SERVINGS
4 PERSONS

INGREDIENTS:

- 2 tsp olive oil
- 1 clove garlic, finely chopped
- 1 tsp red pepper flakes
- 75ml white wine
- 500g cherry tomato
- 300g shrimp
- 350g linguine
- 500ml water
- 1 tsp fine salt
- 50g parmesan, grated

PREPARATIONS:

1. Set the Ninja Foodi to SAUTE and add the olive oil.
2. Then stir in the garlic and red pepper flakes, cook for 1 minute until fragrant.
3. Pour the white wine into the pot and reduce by half.
4. Then add the cherry tomatoes, shrimp, linguine, water and salt.
5. Place the lid on the Ninja Foodi and set to COOK on high pressure for 5 minutes.
6. Release the steam from the pot and stir the ingredients together to combine evenly.
7. Serve the prawn linguine pasta topped with grated parmesan.

BREADED FISH GOUJONS

PREPARATION TIME 10 MINUTES

COOKING TIME 10 MINUTES

SERVINGS 4 PERSONS

INGREDIENTS:
- 450g cod fillets, sliced into strips
- 50g plain flour
- 1 egg, lightly beaten
- 50g breadcrumb
- ½ tsp fine salt
- ½ tsp black pepper
- 2 tsp spray oil

PREPARATIONS:
1. Preheat the Ninja Foodi to COOK at 200C.
2. Into three separate bowls add the plain flour, egg and breadcrumb, season each lightly with salt and black pepper.
3. Dip the cod fillets first into the plain flour then shake off the excess and place into the beaten egg.
4. Finally, toss the cod fillets through the bowl of breadcrumb to coat.
5. Spray the basket of the Ninja Foodi with oil then add the breaded fish goujons in a single layer.
6. Place the basket into the pot then cover with the lid and cook for 5 minutes.
7. Shake the basket to cook the fish goujons evenly then cook for 5 more minutes.

CLAM CHOWDER

PREPARATION TIME 5 MINUTES

COOKING TIME 15 MINUTES

SERVINGS 4 PERSONS

INGREDIENTS:

- 1 tsp olive oil
- 3 slices bacon, diced
- 1 onion, finely chopped
- 1 medium baking potato, diced
- 2 stalk celery, finely chopped
- 1 clove garlic, finely chopped
- 150ml clam juice
- 250ml vegetable stock
- 300g clams
- 500ml single cream
- 75g plain flour
- 2 tbsp parsley, finely chopped

PREPARATIONS:

1. Set the Ninja Foodi to SAUTE and add the olive oil.
2. Stir in the bacon and onion, cook for 2 minutes.
3. Then add the diced potato, celery, garlic, clam juice and vegetable stock.
4. Cover the pot with a lid and program to COOK on high pressure for 5 minutes.
5. Release the steam from the pot then remove the lid.
6. Set the cooker to SAUTE then add the clams and single cream.
7. Sieve the flour into the pot and stir continuously to thicken for a few minutes.
8. Serve the clam chowder topped with parsley and alongside some crusty bread

FRIED SHRIMP

PREPARATION TIME 10 MINUTES

COOKING TIME 5 MINUTES

SERVINGS 4 PERSONS

INGREDIENTS:

- 50g unsalted butter, melted
- 100g breadcrumb
- 2 tsp fajita seasoning
- 1 tsp garlic powder
- ½ tsp onion powder
- ½ tsp cayenne pepper
- 16 jumbo shrimp, peeled with tail-on
- 1 tsp spray oil
- 1 lemon, quartered

PREPARATIONS:

1. Place a saucepan on low heat and add the unsalted butter, allow it to melt.
2. Into a mixing bowl add the breadcrumb, fajita seasoning, garlic powder, onion powder and cayenne pepper.
3. Set the Ninja Foodi to PREHEAT at 200C for 3 minutes.
4. Dip the jumbo shrimp into the melted butter then toss through the mixing bowl of breadcrumbs.
5. Spray the Ninja Foodi basket with spray oil then add the shrimp in a single layer.
6. Place the basket into the Ninja Foodi then set to COOK at 200C.
7. Cook the fried shrimp for 5 minutes until crisp and golden, serve with a wedge of lemon.

TUNA CASSEROLE

PREPARATION TIME 10 MINUTES

COOKING TIME 5 MINUTES

SERVINGS 4 PERSONS

INGREDIENTS:

- 250g egg noodles
- 200g canned tuna, drained
- 100g button mushrooms, sliced
- 75g frozen peas
- 400ml chicken stock
- ½ tsp garlic powder
- ½ tsp fine salt
- 75ml single cream
- 120g cheddar cheese, shredded

PREPARATIONS:

1. Into the Ninja Foodi add the egg noodles, tuna, button mushroom, peas, chicken stock, garlic powder and salt.
2. Stir the ingredients together to evenly combine then cover with the lid.
3. Set the pot to COOK on high pressure for 5 minutes to cook the egg noodles.
4. Release the pressure from the Ninja Foodi then stir in the single cream and cheddar cheese.
5. Serve the tuna casserole whilst hot with extra shredded cheese.

FISH PIE

PREPARATION TIME 10 MINUTES

COOKING TIME 35 MINUTES

SERVINGS 4 PERSONS

INGREDIENTS:

- 800g potatoes, diced
- 250ml water
- 50g unsalted butter
- 75ml milk
- 1 tbsp olive oil
- 1 onion, finely chopped
- 2 tbsp plain flour
- 400ml milk
- 200ml single cream
- 100g peas
- 400g salmon, diced
- 200g haddock, diced
- 75g cheddar cheese, grated

PREPARATIONS:

1. Place the potato into the Ninja Foodi pot and cover with water, season lightly with salt.
2. Cover the pot with a lid then set to COOK on high pressure for 10 minutes.
3. Quick release the pressure then drain off the excess water.
4. Use a potato masher to crush the potatoes then add the butter and milk, mash until a smooth, thick consistency.
5. Transfer the mashed potato to a bowl and keep warm.
6. Clean out the basket of the Ninja Foodi then set to SAUTE.
7. Then add the olive oil and onion, cook for 5 minutes to soften.
8. Stir the flour into the pot and mix continuously for 1 minute.
9. Gradually pour the milk and cream into the pot to form a smooth sauce.
10. Then add the peas, salmon and haddock, spread into an even layer.
11. Top the mixture with the mashed potato and grated cheese.
12. Seal the Ninja Foodi and set to BAKE at 175C for 20 minutes.
13. Release the pressure and serve the fish pie once the top is golden.

SHRIMP BOIL

PREPARATION TIME
15 MINUTES

COOKING TIME
6 MINUTES

SERVINGS
4 PERSONS

INGREDIENTS:

- 1 tbsp unsalted butter
- 2 cloves garlic, finely chopped
- 1 onion, thinly sliced
- 500ml vegetable stock
- 1 tsp Old Bay seasoning
- 1 tsp fine salt
- 400g new potatoes
- 400g Kielbasa sausage, sliced
- 250g sweetcorn
- 400g jumbo shrimp
- 1 tbsp lemon juice

PREPARATIONS:

1. Set the Ninja Foodi to SAUTE and add the butter.
2. Stir in the onion and garlic, cook for 3 minutes to soften.
3. Then add the vegetable stock, Old Bay seasoning and salt, bring the ingredients to a simmer.
4. Lay the new potatoes in a single layer to cover the base of the basket.
5. Next add the sliced sausage and sweetcorn, place the lid on the cooker and set to COOK on high pressure for 5 minutes.
6. Allow a quick release then add the jumbo shrimp into the pot.
7. Close the lid and cook the jumbo shrimp on high pressure for 1 minute.
8. Transfer the shrimp boil to a serving platter then season with fresh lemon juice.

SHRIMP ALFREDO

PREPARATION TIME 10 MINUTES   **COOKING TIME** 8 MINUTES   **SERVINGS** 4 PERSONS

INGREDIENTS:

- 1 tsp vegetable oil
- 1 shallot, finely chopped
- 1 clove garlic, finely chopped
- 350g alfredo sauce
- 200ml water
- 400g fusilli
- 12 jumbo shrimp, peeled and deveined
- 35g mozzarella, shredded
- 50g parmesan, grated

PREPARATIONS:

1. Set the Ninja Foodi to SAUTE and add the vegetable oil.
2. Stir in the shallot and garlic, cook for 5 minutes.
3. Pour the alfredo sauce and water into the pot, mix well.
4. Then add the fusilli and jumbo shrimp ensuring they are covered by liquid.
5. Place the lid onto the Ninja Foodi and set to COOK on high pressure for 3 minutes.
6. Release the pressure for the pot then add the mozzarella and grated parmesan to the shrimp alfredo.

EASY FISH PIE

PREPARATION TIME 10 MINUTES

COOKING TIME 45 MINUTES

SERVINGS 4 PERSONS

INGREDIENTS:

- 2 tbsp cooking oil
- 600 g baby potatoes
- 100 g carrots, peeled and diced
- 1 garlic clove, minced
- 500 g milk
- 1 tbsp butter
- 50 g Cheddar, grated
- 100 g spinach
- 100 g prawns, cleaned and peeled
- 2 whitefish fillets
- 1 tbsp mustard
- 2 cups cooked instant mashed potatoes.
- 2 tbsp parsley, chopped
- Salt and pepper as needed

PREPARATIONS:

1. Season the fish and prawns with salt and pepper and place on the top rack of the Deluxe Reversible Rack. Place in the Ninja Foodi Pressure Cooker Air Fryer with a cup of water.
2. Select the cooking setting for STEAM. Place the pressure cooker lid on and leave the Air Outlet Vent open at the VENT position.
3. Set the timer to 10 minutes. The appliances will warm up, and the countdown timer will begin shortly.
4. Remove the fish and prawns, use a fork to shred the fillets and set them aside.
5. Place the Removable Cooking Pot inside the Pressure Cooker, add the cooking oil, potatoes, carrots and garlic.
6. Select the SEAR/SAUTÉ cooking option with the temperature set to "2". Press START/STOP.
7. Sauté the vegetables until golden (5-10 minutes). Stir regularly.
8. Add the milk, butter, Cheddar and spinach. Incorporate and cook for 10 more minutes until simmering.
9. Add the shredded fish fillet, prawns and mustard. Incorporate and remove from heat.
10. Cover with a layer of warm mashed potatoes.
11. Select the BROIL function and close the Air Fryer lid. Set the temperature to high (390°F 200°C) and the timer to 5-8 minutes.
12. Remove the pot from the appliance, garnish with parsley and serve.

SMOKY FISH GRATIN

PREPARATION TIME
10 MINUTES

COOKING TIME
30 MINUTES

SERVINGS
4 PERSONS

INGREDIENTS:

- 2 tbsp cooking oil
- 1/2 white onion, minced
- 2 garlic cloves, minced
- 2 smoked haddock fillets, diced
- 500 ml milk
- 2 tbsp butter
- 2 tbsp all-purpose flour
- 1 bay leaf
- 166 g Cheddar, grated
- 240 g panko breadcrumbs
- 1 tbsp fresh parsley

PREPARATIONS:

1. Select the SEAR/SAUTÉ cooking option with the temperature set to "2". Press START/STOP.
2. Add the oil into the removable cooking pot and sauté the onion and garlic until golden, fragrant and translucent (5-10 minutes). Stir regularly.
3. Incorporate the haddock and cook until flaky (5 minutes).
4. Add the milk, butter, flour and bay leaf. Incorporate and cook for 10 more minutes until simmering.
5. Cover with a layer of shredded Cheddar and panko crumbs.
6. Select the BROIL function and close the Air Fryer lid. Set the temperature to high (390°F - 200°C) and the timer to 5-8 minutes. Press START/STOP.
7. Remove the pot from the appliance, remove the bay leaf, garnish with parsley and serve.

GARLIC AND HERBS FISH PIE

PREPARATION TIME 10 MINUTES

COOKING TIME 45 MINUTES

SERVINGS 4 PERSONS

INGREDIENTS:

- 4 baking potatoes, diced in 1-inch pieces
- 2 tbsp butter
- 2 tbsp milk
- 2 tbsp chives, chopped
- 2 tbsp butter
- 2 tbsp all-purpose flour
- 2 garlic cloves, minced
- 400 ml milk
- 2 haddock fillets, in cubes
- 100 g peas
- 100 g cream cheese

PREPARATIONS:

1. Place the Deluxe Reversible Rack in the Ninja Foodi Pressure Cooker Air Fryer and place the potatoes on the rack. Add two cups of water and close the Pressure Cooker lid.
2. Select the STEAM cooking mode and set the timer to 16-18 minutes. Press START/STOP.
3. Steam the potatoes until tender. Remove and transfer into a mixing bowl.
4. Mash the potatoes and incorporate the butter, milk and chives. Set aside.
5. Place the removable pot in the Pressure Cooker and add the cooking oil.
6. Set the cooking setting to SEAR/SAUTÉ at a LOW temperature, add the butter and melt. Add the flour while stirring and cook for 1-2 minutes.
7. Add the garlic and sauté until golden.
8. Add the milk gradually and the peas. Allow simmering.
9. Cook the fillets in the milk until flaky. Fold in the cream cheese and mix until thoroughly combined.
10. Top the mixture with the chive mash and change the cooking setting to BROIL.
11. Close the Air Fryer lid. Set the temperature to high (390°F - 200°C) and the timer to 5-8 minutes. Press START/STOP.
12. Once golden, remove from the appliance and serve.

ROAST LAMB WITH GINGER GLAZE

PREPARATION TIME 10 MINUTES

COOKING TIME 55 MINUTES

SERVINGS 4 PERSONS

INGREDIENTS:

- 500 g whole lamb
- 2cm ginger, peeled and minced
- 4 tbsp honey
- 500 g baby potatoes
- 2 rosemary sprigs
- Cooking oil in spray
- Salt and pepper to taste

PREPARATIONS:

1. Spray the lamb with cooking oil and rub with salt and pepper to taste.
2. In a bowl, combine the minced ginger and the honey and brush the lamb.
3. Spray the potatoes with cooking oil and season with salt and pepper.
4. Place the Deluxe Reversible Rack in the Ninja Foodi Pressure Cooker Air Fryer with the potatoes in the bottom and the lamb in the rack's bottom position.
5. Crush the rosemary sprigs and sprinkle over the lamb. Close the Air Frier Lid.
6. Select the function STEAM & CRISP, the temperature at 365°F (185°C) and timer at 45 minutes for medium-rare. Press START/STOP.
7. For more precise cooking, insert the NINJA FOODI SMART THERMOMETER into the lamb aiming at a core temperature of 145°F (63°C).
8. Remove from the appliance, slice the lamb and serve with a side of potatoes.

ROAST LAMB WITH GARLIC

PREPARATION TIME 10 MINUTES

COOKING TIME 55 MINUTES

SERVINGS 4 PERSONS

INGREDIENTS:
- 500 g whole lamb leg
- 2 tbsp flat-leaf parsley
- 2 tbsp butter, melted
- 1 onion, in wedges
- 1 carrot, in large dices
- 1 celery stick, indices
- 2 garlic cloves, minced
- Cooking oil in spray
- Salt and pepper to taste

PREPARATIONS:

1. Brush the lamb with melted butter and rub with salt, pepper and parsley.
2. Combine and spray the onion, carrot, celery and garlic with cooking oil and season with salt and pepper.
3. Place the Deluxe Reversible Rack in the Ninja Foodi Pressure Cooker Air Fryer with the potatoes in the bottom and the lamb in the rack's bottom position. Close the Air Frier Lid.
4. Select the function STEAM & CRISP, the temperature at 365°F (185°C) and timer at 45 minutes for medium-rare. Press START/STOP.
5. For more precise cooking, insert the NINJA FOODI SMART THERMOMETER into the lamb aiming at a core temperature of 145°F (63°C).
6. Remove the lamb and veggies from the appliance, slice the lamb and serve with a side of vegetables.

LAMB AND BEAN HOTPOT

PREPARATION TIME 10 MINUTES

COOKING TIME 55 MINUTES

SERVINGS 4 PERSONS

INGREDIENTS:

- 400 g lean lamb, diced
- 1 tsp all-purpose flour
- 500 g baby potatoes thinly sliced.
- 1 garlic clove, minced
- 1 red onion, in wedges
- 2 leeks, trimmed and sliced
- 2 carrots, peeled and sliced
- 1 bay leaf
- 500 ml beef stock
- 300 g flageolet beans
- Cooking oil in spray

PREPARATIONS:

1. Spray the diced lamb with cooking oil and coat with flour. Set aside.
2. Spray the sliced potatoes and set them aside.
3. Place the lamb, garlic, onion, leeks and carrots in the crisper basket. Place the Deluxe Reversible Rack over the rest of the ingredients and layer the potatoes.
4. Close the air frier lid and select the function AIR FRY. Set the temperature to 390°F and the time to 30 minutes. Press START/STOP.
5. Once the Air Frying is done, carefully remove the Deluxe Reversible Rack and set the crispy potatoes aside.
6. Transfer the contents of the air fryer basket into the Ninja Foodi Pressure Cooker Air Fryer's Removable Cooking Pot and add the bay leaf, beef stock and beans.
7. Place the Pressure Cooker Lid, position the Air Outlet Vent at the SEAL position.
8. Select the PRESSURE setting, set the temperature to HIGH and the timer to 30 minutes. Press START/STOP.
9. Once cooked, Quick Release the pressure in the Air Outlet Vent.
10. Transfer the lamb hot pot into a casserole pot and layer with the crisp potatoes.

BEEF STEW WITH DUMPLINGS

PREPARATION TIME
10 MINUTES

COOKING TIME
35 MINUTES

SERVINGS
4 PERSONS

INGREDIENTS:

Beef Stew
- 1 tbsp vegetable oil
- 500g stewing beef, diced
- 1 onion, finely chopped
- 1 stalk celery, finely chopped
- 150ml stout
- 2 carrots, roughly chopped
- 250g potato, diced
- 1 tbsp cornflour
- 750ml beef stock
- 2 tbsp parsley, finely chopped
- salt, to taste

Dumplings
- 100g self-raising flour
- 50g suet

PREPARATIONS:

1. Set the Ninja Foodi to saute on high heat then add the vegetable oil.
2. Lightly dust the stewing beef in one teaspoon of cornflour then add to the pot, sear for 5 minutes until browned.
3. Remove the beef from the pot and set aside, next add the onion and celery then cook for 5 minutes to soften.
4. Pour the stout into the pot and reduce the volume by half.
5. Next return the beef to the Ninja Foodi along with the carrots, potato and cornflour, stir to combine.
6. Then add the beef stock and place the pressure lid onto the pot, pressure cook on high for 15 minutes.
7. After 15 minutes allow for a natural release for 5 minutes.
8. In a bowl combine the self-raising flour, suet and two tablespoons of water. Use your hands to bring the ingredients together into a dough then shape into eight evenly sized balls.
9. Drop the dumplings into the surface of the beef stew then return the lid to the pot and set to roast at 175C for 15 minutes.
10. Serve the beef stew and dumplings hot, season with salt to taste and garnish with fresh parsley.

ROAST BEEF

PREPARATION TIME 15 MINUTES

COOKING TIME 45 MINUTES

SERVINGS 4 PERSONS

INGREDIENTS:

- 1 tbsp olive oil
- 800g beef roasting joint
- ¼ tsp fine salt
- ¼ tsp black pepper
- 1 onion, thinly sliced
- 2 cloves garlic, finely chopped
- 4 carrots, roughly chopped
- 2 baking potato, roughly chopped
- 120ml beef stock
- 2 tsp Worcestershire sauce

PREPARATIONS:

1. Set the Ninja Foodi to SAUTE and add the olive oil.
2. Season the beef roasting joint with salt and black pepper.
3. Sear the beef in the pot and brown on each side for 2 minutes.
4. Once browned, transfer the beef roasting joint to a plate.
5. Into the Ninja Foodi pot add the onion, garlic, carrots, baking potato, beef stock and Worcestershire sauce.
6. Place the beef roasting joint over the vegetables then cover with the lid.
7. Seal the pot and set to COOK on high pressure for 40 minutes.
8. Naturally release the pressure from the pot then slice the roast beef thinly and serve alongside the cooked vegetables.

SAUSAGE AND ONION GRAVY

PREPARATION TIME 10 MINUTES

COOKING TIME 10 MINUTES

SERVINGS 4 PERSONS

INGREDIENTS:

- 1 tsp olive oil
- 4 onions, thinly sliced
- 400g canned tomatoes
- 200ml beef stock
- ½ tsp cayenne pepper
- ½ tsp fine salt
- 1 tsp black pepper
- 8 Cumberland sausages

PREPARATIONS:

1. Set the Ninja Foodi to SAUTE and add the olive oil.
2. Stir in the sliced onion and cook for 5 minutes to soften.
3. Then add the canned tomatoes, beef stock, cayenne pepper, salt and black pepper, bring the sauce to a simmer.
4. Place the sausages into the sauce and cover the pot with the lid.
5. Set the Ninja Food to COOK on high pressure for 5 minutes.
6. Release the pressure from the pot then remove the sausages, reduce the sauce to form a thick onion gravy.
7. Serve the sausage and onion gravy with mashed potatoes or rice.

CORNED BEEF AND CABBAGE

PREPARATION TIME 10 MINUTES   **COOKING TIME** 60 MINUTES   **SERVINGS** 4 PERSONS

INGREDIENTS:

- 2 medium baking potato, diced
- ½ white cabbage, thinly sliced
- 1 onion
- 650g corned beef
- 250ml beer
- 1 bay leaf

PREPARATIONS:

1. Place the potatoes, cabbage and onion into the base of the Ninja Foodi basket.
2. Lay the corned beef over the potatoes then pour in the beer and bay leaf.
3. Place the lid on the pot and set to COOK on high pressure for 1 hour.
4. Release the steam from the Ninja Foodi then use two forks to shred the corned beef.
5. Serve the corned beef and cabbage hot.

SPRING BEEF AND VEGETABLE HOTPOT

PREPARATION TIME 10 MINUTES

COOKING TIME 30 MINUTES

SERVINGS 4 PERSONS

INGREDIENTS:

- 2 tbsp olive oil
- 500g ground beef
- 1 carrot, peeled and diced
- 1 celery stick, finely chopped
- 1 courgette, diced
- 1 leek, chopped
- 1 garlic clove, minced
- 3 tbsp all-purpose flour
- 1 cup beef stock
- 1 cup tomatoes, chopped
- 1 tbsp Worcestershire sauce
- 1 tbsp fresh thyme
- 400g baby potatoes, sliced

PREPARATIONS:

1. Add one tablespoon of cooking oil into the Ninja Foodi Pressure Cooker Air Fryer inner pot and set to SEAR/SAUTÉ. Adjust temperature to "2". Press START/STOP.
2. Add ground beef and cook until browned. Add in the carrot, celery, courgette, leek and garlic. Cook while stirring often for 5 minutes.
3. Add the flour and cook for one more minute. Add the beef stock, tomatoes, Worcestershire sauce, thyme and potatoes.
4. Place the pressure cooker lid and switch to PRESSURE setting at HIGH temperature. Set the timer to 20 minutes.
5. Adjust the Air Outlet Vent to SEAL and press START/STOP.
6. Quick Release the pressure, remove the lid and serve.

BEEF AND BUTTER BEAN STEW WITH STILTON DUMPLINGS

PREPARATION TIME 10 MINUTES

COOKING TIME 55 MINUTES

SERVINGS 4 PERSONS

INGREDIENTS:

- 1 tbsp all-purpose flour
- 300 g casserole steak, diced
- 1 tbsp cooking oil
- 1 carrot, peeled and diced
- 1 celery stick, chopped
- 1 parsnip, diced
- 1 shallot, minced
- 1 garlic clove, minced
- 200 g beetroot, peeled and diced
- 1 tsp thyme
- 1/2 cup red wine
- 2 cups beef stock
- 1 bay leaf
- 200 g butterbeans
- Salt and pepper to taste
- 60 g Stilton, crumbled

PREPARATIONS:

1. Season the beef chunks with salt and pepper to taste and coat with the all-purpose flour.
2. Add one tablespoon of cooking oil into the Ninja Foodi Pressure Cooker Air Fryer inner pot and set to SEAR/SAUTÉ. Adjust temperature to "2".
3. Add the beef and sear until browned. Add carrot, celery, parsnip, shallot, garlic and beetroot. Cook while stirring often for 5 minutes.
4. Add the beef stock, red wine, thyme, bay leaf and butterbeans.
5. Place the pressure cooker lid and switch to PRESSURE at HIGH temperature.
6. Set the timer to 20 minutes.
7. Adjust the valve to SEAL and press START/STOP.
8. Make sure the KEEP WARM button is turned on.
9. To make the dumplings, combine the flour, thyme, suet and Stilton to form a dough. Shape the dumplings and set them aside.
10. Quick Release the pressure in the pressure cooker, remove the lid and add the dumplings. Cook for 10 more minutes on the KEEP WARM setting.
11. Taste and adjust the seasoning.
12. Discard the bay leaf and serve.

BEEF AND ROOT VEG HOTPOT

PREPARATION TIME 20 MINUTES · **COOKING TIME** 30 MINUTES · **SERVINGS** 4 PERSONS

INGREDIENTS:

- 2 tbsp cooking oil
- 400 g casserole beef, diced
- 1 onion, sliced
- 1 leek, sliced
- 2 carrots, diced
- 1 parsnip, diced
- 1 tbsp flour
- ½ tsp allspice
- 4 tbsp tomato purée
- 100ml red wine
- 1 cup beef stock
- 500g sweet potatoes, peeled and sliced

PREPARATIONS:

1. Add one tablespoon of cooking oil into the Ninja Foodi Pressure Cooker Air Fryer inner pot and set to SEAR/SAUTÉ.
2. Adjust temperature to "2".
3. Add the beef and sear until browned. Add onion, leek, carrot, parsnip, garlic and beetroot. Cook while stirring often for 5 minutes.
4. Add the flour and allspice and cook for one more minute.
5. Add the beef stock, red wine, tomato purée and sweet potatoes.
6. Place the pressure cooker lid and switch to PRESSURE at HIGH temperature.
7. Set the timer to 20 minutes.
8. Adjust the Air Outlet Vent to SEAL and press START/STOP.
9. Once the time has passed, Quick Release the pressure, remove the lid.
10. Taste and adjust the seasoning.
11. Serve while still hot.

LEFTOVER PORK SANDWICHES WITH APPLE SLAW

PREPARATION TIME 10 MINUTES

COOKING TIME 55 MINUTES

SERVINGS 4 PERSONS

For the slaw:

- 3 cups chopped cabbage
- 2 red apples, cored and chopped
- 1 carrot, grated
- ½ cup finely chopped red bell pepper
- 2 green onions, chopped
- ⅓ cup mayonnaise
- ⅓ cup brown sugar
- 1 tbsp lemon juice

For the sandwiches:

- 4 sourdough buns
- 400 g cooked crackling pork loin joint, sliced
- 2 tbsp mustard
- 4 slices cheddar cheese

PREPARATIONS:

1. To make the slaw, combine the cabbage, apple, carrot, bell pepper, onions, mayonnaise, brown sugar and lemon juice in a bowl. Toss to combine and marinate for at least 20 minutes before serving.
2. For the sandwiches, spread the crackling pork loin join on the Ninja Foodi Pressure Cooker Air Fryer's Deluxe Reversible Rack and place inside the appliance.
3. Adjust the setting to BAKE/ROAST, the temperature to 200°F (93°C) and the timer to 5 minutes. Close the lid with the Air Outlet Vent set to VENT and press START/STOP.
4. Remove the crackling pork loin joint and place the sourdough buns on the racks. Close the lid and allow the residual heat to warm the buns for 2-3 minutes.
5. Cut the buns in half, stuff with pork, top with cheese, and spread the top bun with mustard.
6. Serve with apple slaw and enjoy.

LEEK RAREBIT PORK STEAKS

PREPARATION TIME 10 MINUTES   **COOKING TIME** 50 MINUTES   **SERVINGS** 4 PERSONS

INGREDIENTS:

- 3 large leeks, trimmed and sliced
- 120 g mature Cheddar, grated
- 1 tsp English mustard
- 4 pork loin steaks
- 2 tbsp cooking oil
- Salt and pepper to taste

PREPARATIONS:

1. To steam the leeks, arrange the sliced leeks on the Deluxe Reversible Rack and place them in the Ninja Foodi Pressure Cooker Air Fryer with one cup of water.
2. Place the Pressure Cooker lid. Leave the Air Outlet Vent open at the VENT position.
3. Select the cooking setting to steam and set the timer to 10 minutes. Press START/STOP; The appliance will preheat before starting the countdown.
4. Once the leeks are done, transfer them into a mixing bowl and immediately toss with the grated Cheddar and mustard. Season with salt and pepper and keep in a warm place.
5. To air-fry the pork loin steaks, rub them with cooking oil and place them on the Deluxe Reversible Rack in the Ninja Foodi Pressure Cooker Air Fryer.
6. Close the Air-Frying lid, select the AIR-FRY function, adjust the temperature to 375°F and set the timer to 30 minutes.
7. Once fully cooked and crispy, serve the pork loin steaks with a side of cheesy leeks.

MUSHROOM AND CREAMY MUSTARD PORK STEAKS

PREPARATION TIME 10 MINUTES

COOKING TIME 50 MINUTES

SERVINGS 4 PERSONS

INGREDIENTS:

- 1 tbsp cooking oil
- 4 pork loin steaks
- 380 g mushrooms, sliced
- 1 garlic clove, crushed
- 2 tbsp Dijon mustard
- 150 ml double cream
- 100 ml chicken stock
- 2 tbsp parsley, chopped

PREPARATIONS:

1. Rub the loin steaks with cooking oil, place them on the Deluxe Reversible Rack in the Ninja Foodi Pressure Cooker Air Fryer, and set them to AIRFRY.
2. Adjust temperature to 375°F (190°C). Set the timer to 15-17 minutes.
3. Once air-fried, set the pork loin aside.
4. Add one tablespoon of cooking oil into the Ninja Foodi Pressure Cooker Air Fryer inner pot and set to SEAR/SAUTÉ. Adjust temperature to "2". Press START/STOP.
5. Add the mushrooms and sauté until the excess water evaporates.
6. Add the garlic, Dijon, double cream and chicken stock. Stir to combine.
7. Cook for 10 minutes with the lid down.
8. Add the loin steaks back and cook for 5 more minutes with the lid off.
9. Serve and garnish with parsley.

SWEET AND SOUR PORK

PREPARATION TIME 20 MINUTES

COOKING TIME 20 MINUTES

SERVINGS 4 PERSONS

INGREDIENTS:

- 1 tbsp vegetable oil
- 500g pork fillet, diced
- 2 tbsp cornflour
- 1 red onion, diced
- 1 red pepper, diced
- 2 cloves garlic, finely chopped
- 4 tbsp rice vinegar
- 2 tbsp tomato ketchup
- 2 tbsp soy sauce
- 2 tbsp brown sugar
- 100ml water / pineapple juice
- 150g pineapple, diced
- 2 tbsp spring onions, thinly sliced
- salt, to taste

PREPARATIONS:

1. Set the Ninja Foodi to saute and select medium heat then pour in the vegetable oil.
2. In a bowl toss together the diced pork fillet, cornflour and salt then add the coated pork into the pressure cooker.
3. Saute the pork for 5 minutes until browned on all sides then remove and set aside.
4. Into the pressure cooker add the red onion, red pepper and garlic, saute for 2 minutes.
5. Then pour in the rice vinegar, tomato ketchup, soy sauce, brown sugar, water and diced pineapple, bring the sauce to a simmer and stir to combine.
6. Return the browned pork to the pot then cover with the pressure lid and turn the back valve to seal. Set to pressure cook on high for 10 minutes then quick-release pressure.
7. Serve the sweet and sour pork garnished with thinly sliced spring onions.

SICHUAN PEPPERCORN STEAK

PREPARATION TIME 15 MINUTES

COOKING TIME 5 MINUTES

SERVINGS 4 PERSONS

INGREDIENTS:

- 2 tsp olive oil
- 400g sirloin steak, sliced into strips
- 2 cloves garlic, finely chopped
- 1 tsp Sichuan peppercorns, crushed
- ½ tsp ground black pepper
- ¼ tsp fine salt
- 2 tsp hoisin sauce
- 2 tsp brown sugar
- 1 red bell pepper, sliced into strips
- 2 tbsp cornflour
- 100ml beef stock
- 8 spring onions, thinly sliced

PREPARATIONS:

1. Set the Ninja Foodi to SAUTE and add the olive oil.
2. Sear the steak strips in the pot for 2 minutes until browned.
3. Then add the garlic and sichuan peppercorns, cook for 1 minute.
4. Stir the ground black pepper, salt, hoisin sauce, brown sugar and bell peppers to form a sauce.
5. In a bowl whisk together the cornflour and beef stock then pour into the pot.
6. Place the lid onto the Ninja Foodi then set to COOK on high pressure for 3 minutes.
7. Release the pressure from the pot then serve the sichuan peppercorn stock over rice, topped with spring onions.

CHILI VERDE

PREPARATION TIME 15 MINUTES

COOKING TIME 45 MINUTES

SERVINGS 4 PERSONS

INGREDIENTS:
- 1 tbsp olive oil
- 800g pork loin, diced into 1-inch pieces
- 200ml vegetable stock
- 200g green enchilada sauce
- 1 onion, finely chopped
- 250g green jalapenos, roughly chopped

PREPARATIONS:
1. Set the Ninja Foodi to SAUTE and add the olive oil.
2. Then add the diced pork loin, sear for 5 minutes until browned.
3. Pour the vegetable stock into the pot and scrape the base to deglaze.
4. Turn off the Ninja Foodi then add the green enchilada sauce and onion.
5. Close the lid to the pot then set to COOK on high pressure for 30 minutes.
6. Allow for a quick release of pressure then stir in the green jalapenos.
7. Cook the chili verde for a further 10 minutes then serve.

CHICKEN AND HERB BAKE WITH TOMATOES

PREPARATION TIME 10 MINUTES

COOKING TIME 25 MINUTES

SERVINGS 4 PERSONS

INGREDIENTS:

- 4 chicken breasts, boneless, skinless
- 6 tbsp cream cheese
- 1 tbsp dried cooking herbs
- 1 tbsp panko breadcrumbs
- 250 g cherry tomatoes
- Cooking oil in spray
- Salt and pepper to taste
- 2 tbsp basil, chopped

PREPARATIONS:

1. Combine the cream cheese and the cooking herbs.
2. Brush the chicken breasts with oil, spread the herb cream cheese over the chicken breasts, and top them with breadcrumbs.
3. Spray the tomatoes with cooking oil and season with salt and pepper.
4. Place the Deluxe Reversible Rack inside the Ninja Foodi Pressure Cooker Air Fryer.
5. Place the tomatoes on the bottom along with half a cup of water and the chicken breasts arranged on the racks.
6. Close the Air Fryer lid. Select the cooking setting STEAM & CRISP. Adjust the temperature to 385°F (196°C) and the timer to 15-20 minutes. Press START/STOP.
7. Allow the appliance to steam and crisp the chicken and tomatoes. Carefully remove the rack, garnish with basil and serve.

SPRING ROASTED CHICKEN WITH TARRAGON

PREPARATION TIME 10 MINUTES

COOKING TIME 80 MINUTES

SERVINGS 4 PERSONS

INGREDIENTS:

- 1 whole chicken
- 4 tbsp butter, softened
- 1 tbsp fresh tarragon
- 1 tbsp fresh thyme
- 300 g shallots, halved
- 1 garlic clove, crushed

PREPARATIONS:

1. Rub the chicken with softened butter and coat with the tarragon and thyme.
2. Place the chicken in the Steam and Crisp Basket along with one cup of water.
3. Place the shallots and garlic around the chicken.
4. Close the Ninja Foodi Pressure Cooker Air Fryer's Air Fryer lid. Select the cooking setting STEAM & CRISP. Adjust the temperature to 365°F (185°C) and the timer to 60-80 minutes. Press START/STOP.
5. Allow the appliance to steam and crisp the chicken. Check if cooked through at the 60-minute mark.
6. Carefully remove the Steam and Crisp Basket, carve and serve with a side of shallots.

STICKY CHICKEN WINGS

PREPARATION TIME
5 MINUTES

COOKING TIME
30 MINUTES

SERVINGS
4 PERSONS

INGREDIENTS:
- 500 g chicken wings
- 4 tbsp soy sauce
- 1/4 tbsp honey
- 2 tbsp ketchup
- 1/2 tsp garlic powder
- 1/2 tsp ground ginger

PREPARATIONS:

1. Combine the soy sauce, honey, ketchup, garlic powder and ground ginger in a mixing bowl.
2. Toss the wings in the glaze and drip off the excess sauce.
3. Place the Deluxe Reversible Rack in the Ninja Foodi Pressure Cooker Air Fryer and arrange the chicken wings on both racks.
4. Close the Air Fryer lid and set the cooking to AIR FRY, the temperature to 390°F (200°C) and the timer to 24–28 minutes. Press START/STOP.
5. Serve immediately with a blue cheese dip.

SUNDAY ROAST CHICKEN

PREPARATION TIME
15 MINUTES

COOKING TIME
60 MINUTES

SERVINGS
4 PERSONS

INGREDIENTS:

- 1.5kg whole chicken
- 1 lemon, halved
- 3 sprigs rosemary
- 5 sprigs thyme
- 25g unsalted butter, room temperature
- 250ml chicken stock
- salt, to taste
- black pepper, to taste

PREPARATIONS:

1. Place the double layer rack into the inner pot of the Ninja Foodi then pour in the chicken stock.
2. Into the cavity of the chicken add the two lemon halves, rosemary, thyme, salt and black pepper.
3. Brush the chicken skin with softened butter then season with salt and black pepper.
4. Place the whole chicken onto the double layer rack in the Ninja Foodi and seal with the lid.
5. Set to pressure cook on high for 35 minutes.
6. After 35 minutes, allow for a quick release and remove the lid.
7. Lift the chicken and pour any juices from inside the cavity into the base of the pot.
8. Place the air crisp lid on the pot and set to air crisp at 200C for 20 minutes.
9. Once the chicken skin becomes golden and crisp, transfer from the pot to a chopping board.
10. Remove the lemon, rosemary and thyme from the cavity and discard.
11. Allow the Sunday roast chicken to rest for 5 minutes before serving.

CHICKEN TACO BOWL

PREPARATION TIME 10 MINUTES

COOKING TIME 15 MINUTES

SERVINGS 4 PERSONS

INGREDIENTS:
- 2 tsp olive oil
- 400g chicken breast
- 200ml chicken stock
- 100g sweetcorn
- 100g canned black beans, drained
- 100g rice
- 1 tsp taco seasoning
- 4 tbsp sour cream
- 25g tortilla chips
- 25g Monterey Jack cheese, shredded

PREPARATIONS:

1. Set the Ninja Foodi Pressure Cooker to SAUTE and add the olive oil.
2. Place the chicken breast into the pot and sear for 2 minutes.
3. Then flip the chicken and sear for a further 2 minutes.
4. Pour the chicken stock into the pot and bring to a gentle simmer.
5. Then add the sweetcorn, black beans, rice and taco seasoning.
6. Cover the cooker with the lid and seal, set to COOK on high for 10 minutes.
7. Release the steam from the cooker and remove the lid, use two forks to shred the chicken breast.
8. Transfer the chicken taco mixture into four bowls then top with sour cream, tortilla chips and shredded cheese.

CHICKEN FAJITAS

PREPARATION TIME 10 MINUTES

COOKING TIME 20 MINUTES

SERVINGS 4 PERSONS

INGREDIENTS:

- 400g chicken thigh, sliced into strips
- 1 red bell pepper, diced
- 1 green bell pepper, diced
- 1 red onion, diced
- 2 tsp fajita seasoning
- 1 tsp spray oil
- 4 flour tortillas
- 1 avocado, sliced

PREPARATIONS:

1. Spray the Ninja Foodi pressure cooker and air fryer basket with oil.
2. Place the chicken thigh, red bell pepper, green bell pepper, red onion and fajita seasoning into the basket.
3. Place the basket into the air fryer and set it to COOK at 180C for 10 minutes.
4. Then remove the basket and mix the ingredients to ensure even cooking, return the basket and cook for 10 more minutes.
5. Divide the cooked chicken fajita mixture between the four tortillas then top each with sliced avocado.
6. Tightly wrap the chicken fajitas then serve.

SPATCHCOCK CHICKEN

PREPARATION TIME
5 MINUTES

COOKING TIME
25 MINUTES

SERVINGS
4 PERSONS

INGREDIENTS:
- 1.5kg chicken
- 500g new potatoes, halved
- 2 tbsp olive oil
- 1 sprig rosemary
- 3 sprig thyme
- 1 clove garlic
- 1 lemon, halved
- ½ tsp fine salt
- ½ tsp black pepper

PREPARATIONS:

1. Slice the chicken to remove the spine then press down to flatten.
2. Season the chicken with olive oil, salt and black pepper.
3. Place the new potatoes into the Ninja Foodi basket then cover with 100ml water.
4. Lay the grill rack into the basket then add the spatchcock chicken.
5. Then add the rosemary, thyme, garlic and lemon into the Ninja Foodi.
6. Cover the pot with the lid and set to COOK at 180C for 20 minutes.
7. Release the pressure from the Ninja Foodi and allow the spatchcock chicken to rest for 5 minutes.
8. Serve the chicken alongside the new potatoes.

CHICKEN AND MUSHROOM RISOTTO

PREPARATION TIME
15 MINUTES

COOKING TIME
10 MINUTES

SERVINGS
4 PERSONS

INGREDIENTS:

- 2 tbsp olive oil
- 1 onion, finely chopped
- 200g chestnut mushroom, thinly sliced
- 1 clove garlic, finely chopped
- 450g chicken breast, diced
- 400g arborio rice
- 900ml chicken stock
- 1 tsp thyme
- 50g unsalted butter
- 100g parmesan cheese, grated

PREPARATIONS:

1. Set the Ninja Foodi to SAUTE and add the olive oil.
2. Stir in the chopped onion and cook for 5 minutes until translucent.
3. Then add the mushroom and garlic to the pot, cook for 3 minutes.
4. Next add the diced chicken breast, mix through with the mushroom and onion.
5. Turn off the Ninja Foodi and deglaze with a splash of chicken stock.
6. Then add the arborio rice, thyme and remaining chicken stock.
7. Place the lid on the pot and set to COOK of high pressure for 4 minutes.
8. Allow the risotto to rest for 6 minutes then release the pressure.
9. Fold the butter and parmesan chicken into the chicken and mushroom risotto then serve.

CHICKEN SATAY

PREPARATION TIME 10 MINUTES

COOKING TIME 10 MINUTES

SERVINGS 4 PERSONS

INGREDIENTS:

- 1 tbsp peanut oil
- 2 chicken breast, diced
- 75ml chicken stock
- 255ml coconut milk
- 2 tbsp soy sauce
- 1 tbsp palm sugar
- ½ tsp ground ginger
- ½ tsp garlic powder
- 1 tbsp lime juice
- 100g smooth peanut butter
- ½ tsp cornflour
- 25g peanuts, crushed
- 2 tbsp coriander, finely chopped
-

PREPARATIONS:

1. Set the Ninja Foodi to SAUTE and add the peanut oil.
2. Then add the diced chicken breast and cook for 5 minutes until well browned.
3. Pour the chicken stock into the pot and scrape the base to deglaze.
4. Turn off the pot then add the coconut milk, soy sauce, palm sugar, ground ginger, garlic powder, lime juice and peanut butter, stir together to combine evenly.
5. Place a lid on the pot then set to COOK on high pressure for 6 minutes, then allow a natural release of pressure.
6. Whisk together the cornflour and one teaspoon of water then pour into the chicken satay and stir through.
7. Once the chicken satay has thickened, top with crushed peanuts and chopped coriander.

STUFFED COURGETTES WITH ROCKET SALAD

PREPARATION TIME 10 MINUTES

COOKING TIME 15 MINUTES

SERVINGS 4 PERSONS

INGREDIENTS:

- 4 large courgettes
- 50 g onion, minced
- 2 garlic cloves, crushed
- 400 g tomato paste
- 125 g mozzarella, sliced
- 4 tbsp panko breadcrumbs
- Cooking oil in spray
- Salt and pepper to taste
- 2 tbsp basil leaves for garnish

For the salad

- 100 g rocket, shredded
- 2 tbsp red wine vinegar
- 2 tbsp olive oil
- 1 tsp crushed pepper flakes

PREPARATIONS:

1. Cut the courgettes in half and hollow without piercing. Spray with cooking oil.
2. In a mixing bowl, combine the onion, garlic and tomato paste. Fill the courgette halves.
3. Top each courgette with mozzarella and panko breadcrumbs.
4. Place the Deluxe Reversible Rack in the Ninja Foodi Pressure Cooker Air Fryer and arrange the courgette halves on both racks.
5. Close the Air Fryer lid and set the cooking to AIR FRY, the temperature to 390°F (200°C) and the timer to 10-12 minutes. Press START/STOP.
6. To assemble the salad, toss the rocket with vinegar, olive oil and red pepper flakes. Set aside.
7. Serve the courgettes and garnish with drizzled olive oil, basil leaves and a side of rocket salad.

RAW KALE TABBOULEH WITH FRIED HALLOUMI

PREPARATION TIME 10 MINUTES

COOKING TIME 25 MINUTES

SERVINGS 4 PERSONS

INGREDIENTS:
- 1 tbsp olive oil
- 200 g bulgur wheat
- 1 shallot, minced
- 100 g kale, chopped
- 1/2 cucumber, sliced thinly
- 1 lemon, juice and zest
- 50 g fresh mint
- 50 g fresh flat-leaf parsley
- Salt and pepper to taste
- Olive oil for drizzling
- 225 g of halloumi, in thick slices

PREPARATIONS:

1. Place the bulgur heat with one cup of water in the Ninja Foodi Pressure Cooker Air Fryer. Close the Pressure Cooker lid and select the STEAM cooking setting. Make sure the Air Outlet Vent is in the VENT position.
2. Select the timer to 2 minutes. Press START/STOP.
3. Ensure the KEEP WARM setting is on.
4. Once the two minutes have passed, allow the bulgur wheat to rest for 10 minutes. Scoop out and transfer into a mixing bowl.
5. Combine the bulgur wheat with the shallot, kale, cucumber, lemon juice and zest, mint and parsley. Season with salt and pepper and drizzle with olive oil. Toss to coat.
6. Place the Deluxe Reversible Rack in the Ninja Foodi Pressure Cooker Air Fryer and arrange the halloumi slices on both racks.
7. Close the Air Fryer lid and set the cooking to AIR FRY, the temperature to 390°F (200°C) and the timer to 8-10 minutes. Press START/STOP.
8. Serve the tabbouleh and top it with the crispy halloumi.

BUFFALO CAULIFLOWER BITES

PREPARATION TIME 5 MINUTES

COOKING TIME 15 MINUTES

SERVINGS 4 PERSONS

INGREDIENTS:

- 2 tbsp unsalted butter, melted
- 75ml buffalo sauce
- 1 cauliflower, broken into florets
- 70g breadcrumbs
- 2 tsp garlic powder
- ½ tsp fine salt
- ½ tsp black pepper
- 1 tsp spray oil

PREPARATIONS:

1. Into a mixing bowl add the melted butter and buffalo sauce, whisk together.
2. Then add the cauliflower florets and toss through to coat in the sauce.
3. In a second bowl, combine the breadcrumbs, garlic powder, salt and black pepper.
4. Transfer the cauliflower florets into the bowl of breadcrumbs and mix.
5. Spray the Ninja Foodi basket with spray oil then add the buffalo cauliflower bites.
6. Set the pot to 170C and cook for 12 minutes until crisp and golden.
7. Serve the buffalo cauliflower bites with extra buffalo sauce.

MASHED POTATO

PREPARATION TIME 15 MINUTES

COOKING TIME 5 MINUTES

SERVINGS 4 PERSONS

INGREDIENTS:

- 4 King Edward potatoes, peeled and roughly chopped
- 25g unsalted butter, room temperature
- 100ml milk
- 50ml single cream
- ½ tsp garlic powder
- ¼ tsp fine salt
- ¼ tsp ground black pepper

PREPARATIONS:

1. Place the chopped potatoes into the Ninja Foodi pot and cover with water.
2. Cover the pot with the lid and set to COOK on high pressure for 5 minutes.
3. Release the pressure from the pot and pour away any excess water.
4. Use a potato masher to crush the potatoes until smooth.
5. Then add the butter, milk, cream, garlic powder and salt, continue to use the potato masher to form a smooth, silky texture.
6. Adjust the consistency with extra milk then serve the mashed potato.

MUSHROOM RISOTTO

PREPARATION TIME 10 MINUTES

COOKING TIME 20 MINUTES

SERVINGS 4 PERSONS

INGREDIENTS:

- 1 tbsp unsalted butter
- 1 shallot, finely diced
- 1 clove garlic, finely grated
- 500g chestnut mushroom, thinly sliced
- 320g arborio rice
- 100ml white wine
- 1L vegetable stock
- 70g parmesan cheese, grated
- salt, to taste

PREPARATIONS:

1. Set the Ninja Foodi to saute on high then add the unsalted butter.
2. Once the butter has melted, stir in the diced shallot and cook for 5 minutes to soften.
3. Then add the garlic and mushrooms, cook for a further 5 minutes.
4. Stir the arborio rice into the pot and mix continuously to lightly toast for 1 minutes.
5. Pour in the white wine and reduce by half then add the vegetable stock.
6. Place the pressure lid onto the pot and seal, set to pressure cook on high for 8 minutes.
7. Then allow for a natural release to reveal the perfectly cooked risotto, season with salt to taste.
8. Stir the grated parmesan into the mushroom risotto and serve warm.

LEEK AND POTATO SOUP

PREPARATION TIME 15 MINUTES

COOKING TIME 30 MINUTES

SERVINGS 4 PERSONS

INGREDIENTS:

- 2 tbsp unsalted butter
- 1 leek, thinly sliced
- 1 clove garlic, thinly sliced
- 1kg Maris piper potatoes, peeled and roughly chopped
- 500ml chicken stock / vegetable stock
- 200ml double cream
- 1 tbsp chives, finely chopped
- salt, to taste
- black pepper, to taste

PREPARATIONS:

1. Heat the inner pot of the Ninja Food by setting to saute on medium, add the unsalted butter.
2. Then add the sliced leek and cook for 5 minutes to soften.
3. Next add the garlic and chopped potatoes, cook for 3 minutes.
4. Pour the chicken stock into the pot and bring to a simmer.
5. Place the pressure lid onto the pot and seal, set to pressure cook for 10 minutes.
6. After 10 minutes, allow the pot to natural release for 5 minutes.
7. Remove the pressure lid from the Ninja Foodi and crush the softened vegetables using a potato masher.
8. Then add the double cream to form a thick soup consistency, adjust with extra cream or chicken stock to your liking.
9. Season the leek and potato soup with salt and black pepper then serve garnished with chopped chives.

STEAMED BROCCOLI

PREPARATION TIME
5 MINUTES

COOKING TIME
5 MINUTES

SERVINGS
4 PERSONS

INGREDIENTS:

- 1 head broccoli, broken into florets
- 500ml water
- 1 tsp fine salt

PREPARATIONS:

1. Break the head of broccoli into florets.
2. Pour the water and salt into the basket of the Ninja Foodi.
3. Place the broccoli florets into the inner basket then close the lid of the pot.
4. Set the Ninja Foodi to STEAM for 5 minutes.
5. Release the pressure from the pot then serve the steamed broccoli.

ROASTED ROOT VEGETABLES

PREPARATION TIME 10 MINUTES

COOKING TIME 15 MINUTES

SERVINGS 4 PERSONS

INGREDIENTS:

- 2 red onion, roughly chopped
- 3 carrot, roughly chopped
- 2 parsnip, roughly chopped
- ¼ celeriac, roughly chopped
- 1 tsp smoked paprika
- 1 tsp garlic powder
- 1 tsp thyme
- ½ tsp fine salt
- ½ tsp black pepper
- 1 tbsp olive oil

PREPARATIONS:

1. Into a mixing bowl add the red onion, carrot, parsnip and celeriac.
2. Season the root vegetables with smoked paprika, garlic powder, thyme, salt, black pepper and olive oil.
3. Preheat the Ninja Foodi to 200C for 5 minutes.
4. Place the root vegetables into the basket then cover with the lid.
5. Set the Ninja Foodi to COOK on high pressure for 15 minutes, shake after 5 minutes to ensure even cooking.
6. Serve the roasted root vegetables once crisp and browned.

TATER TOTS

PREPARATION TIME
5 MINUTES

COOKING TIME
20 MINUTES

SERVINGS
4 PERSONS

INGREDIENTS:

- 400g frozen tater tots
- 50g mozzarella, shredded
- 1 tsp spray oil

PREPARATIONS:

1. Set the Ninja Foodi to preheat at 200C for 5 minutes.
2. Grease the basket with spray oil then add the frozen tater tots.
3. Place the tater tots into the pot and cook for 5 minutes.
4. Then remove the basket and shake well, return the basket to the pot for 5 more minutes.
5. Repeat this process one more time until the tater tots and crisp and golden.
6. Then sprinkle the shredded mozzarella over the tater tots and cook for a further 2 minutes to melt the cheese, serve immediately.

FRIED CABBAGE

PREPARATION TIME 10 MINUTES

COOKING TIME 10 MINUTES

SERVINGS 4 PERSONS

INGREDIENTS:

- 1 tbsp olive oil
- 100g bacon, diced
- 1 onion, finely chopped
- 1 medium cabbage, shredded
- 200ml vegetable stock
- ½ tsp garlic powder
- ½ tsp fine salt
- ½ tsp smoked paprika
- ¼ tsp cayenne pepper

PREPARATIONS:

1. Set the Ninja Foodi to SAUTE and add the olive oil.
2. Stir in the diced bacon and onion, cook for 3 minutes.
3. Then add the shredded cabbage to the pot and stir through.
4. Pour in the vegetable stock then add the garlic powder, salt, smoked paprika and cayenne pepper.
5. Place the lid onto the Ninja Foodi then set to high pressure for 5 minutes.
6. Release the pressure from the pot then serve the fried cabbage.

POTATO SALAD

PREPARATION TIME
15 MINUTES

COOKING TIME
5 MINUTES

SERVINGS
4 PERSONS

INGREDIENTS:

- 500g red potato, diced
- 2 shallots, finely chopped
- 2 tsp capers, finely chopped
- 1 tbsp gherkins, finely chopped
- 50g mayonnaise
- 1 tbsp white wine vinegar
- 2 tsp Dijon mustard
- 2 tbsp chives, finely chopped

PREPARATIONS:

1. Pour 500ml of water into the basket of the Ninja Foodi pot.
2. Place the diced red potato into the basket then cover with the lid.
3. Set to COOK for 5 minutes until the potatoes are tender.
4. Release the steam from the pot then strain off any excess water.
5. Lightly crush the potatoes in the basket with a fork.
6. Stir the shallots, capers, gherkins, mayonnaise, white wine vinegar, mustard and chives into the potatoes.
7. Transfer the potato salad to a bowl and chill in the refrigerator before serving.

LENTIL SOUP

PREPARATION TIME 10 MINUTES

COOKING TIME 30 MINUTES

SERVINGS 4 PERSONS

INGREDIENTS:

- 1 tsp olive oil
- 1 onions, finely chopped
- 2 stalk celery, finely chopped
- 1 carrot, finely chopped
- 1 clove garlic, finely chopped
- 120g dry lentils
- 500ml vegetable stock
- ½ tsp fine salt
- 2 tbsp parsley, finely chopped

PREPARATIONS:

1. Set the Ninja Foodi to SAUTE and add the olive oil.
2. Stir in the onion, celery, carrot and garlic, cook for 5 minutes.
3. Then add the dry lentils, vegetable stock and salt to the pot.
4. Place the lid on the pot and set to COOK on high pressure for 25 minutes.
5. Allow a slow release of pressure from the Ninja Foodi then add the parsley.
6. Adjust the consistency of the lentil soup with extra water then serve.

COURGETTE FRITTI

PREPARATION TIME
10 MINUTES

COOKING TIME
15 MINUTES

SERVINGS
4 PERSONS

INGREDIENTS:

- 3 courgette
- 200g panko breadcrumb
- 1 tsp garlic powder
- 1 tsp onion powder
- ½ tsp fine salt
- 1 egg, lightly beaten
- 1 tbsp spray oil

PREPARATIONS:

Slice the courgette into long french fry chips.
Into a mixing bowl add the panko breadcrumb, garlic powder, onion powder and salt.
Dip the courgette into the beaten egg then toss into the bowl of seasoned breadcrumbs.
Spray the Ninja Foodi basket with spray oil then add the courgette fritti in a single layer.
Place the basket into the Ninja Foodi then set it to COOK at 180C for 10 minutes.
Shake the basket to ensure even cooking then cook the courgette for 5 more minutes.
Serve the crispy, golden brown courgette fritti immediately.

BAKED POTATOES

PREPARATION TIME
5 MINUTES

COOKING TIME
15 MINUTES

SERVINGS
4 PERSONS

INGREDIENTS:

- 4 medium potatoes
- ½ tsp fine salt
- 6 spring onions, thinly sliced
- 100g cheddar cheese, grated

PREPARATIONS:

1. Scrub the potato skins clean then pierce the potatoes several times with a sharp knife to allow steam to escape whilst cooking.
2. Season the potatoes with salt then place onto a trivet with the basket of the Ninja Foodi.
3. Pour 250ml water into the base of the basket then cover with the lid.
4. Set the Ninja Foodi to COOK on high pressure for 15 minutes.
5. Release the pressure from the pot then remove the potatoes.
6. Slice the potatoes through the middle to expose the cooked flesh.
7. Top each baked potato with spring onions and cheddar cheese then serve.

CHOCOLATE MOUSSE

PREPARATION TIME 10 MINUTES

COOKING TIME 10 MINUTES

SERVINGS 4 PERSONS

INGREDIENTS:

- 4 egg yolks, lightly beaten
- 160g icing sugar
- 50ml water
- 25g cocoa powder
- 250ml whipping cream
- 125ml milk
- ½ tsp vanilla extract

PREPARATIONS:

1. Place a saucepan on low heat and add the icing sugar, water and cocoa powder.
2. Whisk the ingredients to dissolve the sugar and bring into a smooth paste.
3. Pour the whipping cream, milk and vanilla extract into the saucepan and warm through.
4. Remove the saucepan on warm cream from the heat then pour a tablespoon of the mixture into the bowl of egg yolks, whisk together.
5. Continue to gradually pour the cream into the egg yolks, whisk continuously.
6. Divide the chocolate mousse mixture between four ramekins.
7. Place the ramekins into the Ninja Foodi pot over a trivet then pour 200ml water around the ramekins.
8. Cover the Ninja Foodi with the lid and seal, set to COOK for 5 minutes.
9. Release the pressure from the pot and transfer the ramekins to the refrigerator.
10. Allow the chocolate mousse to chill in the fridge for 2 hours before serving.

RICE PUDDING

PREPARATION TIME 10 MINUTES

COOKING TIME 15 MINUTES

SERVINGS 4 PERSONS

INGREDIENTS:

- 100g pudding rice
- 600ml milk
- 70g caster sugar
- ½ tsp ground cinnamon
- 200ml double cream
- 2 tbsp honey
- 8 strawberries, diced

PREPARATIONS:

1. Into the inner pot of the Ninja Foodi add the pudding rice, milk, caster sugar and ground cinnamon.
2. Place the pressure lid onto the pot and seal, then set to pressure cook on high for 10 minutes.
3. After 10 minutes, allow the pot to naturally release pressure for 3 minutes and remove the lid.
4. While the rice pudding is warm, add the double cream and fold through until thick and creamy.
5. Serve the rice pudding topped with diced strawberries then drizzle over honey.

CHOCOLATE BROWNIES

PREPARATION TIME
15 MINUTES

COOKING TIME
45 MINUTES

SERVINGS
4 PERSONS

INGREDIENTS:

- 2 eggs, lightly beaten
- 75g caster sugar
- 50g brown sugar
- 2 tsp vanilla extract
- 150g chocolate chips, melted
- 150g unsalted butter, melted
- 75g plain flour
- 25g cocoa powder
- ½ tsp salt

PREPARATIONS:

1. Lightly grease a baking dish with one tablespoon of butter.
2. Into a mixing bowl add the eggs, caster sugar, brown sugar and vanilla extract, whisk to combine.
3. Next pour in the melted chocolate and melted butter, continue to whisk until the mixture is smooth.
4. Then in a second mixing bowl stir together the plain flour, cocoa powder and salt.
5. Gradually add the bowl of dry ingredients into the bowl of wet ingredients, fold together until evenly combined.
6. Pour the brownie mixture into the prepared baking dish.
7. Insert the double layer rack into the inner pot of the Ninja Foodi and lay the baking dish on top, set the machine to air fry at 160C for 45 minutes.
8. Test the chocolate brownies by inserting a skewer into the centre, if it comes out clean then the brownies are ready whereas if it has some batter on the skewer cook for a further 5 minutes.
9. Allow the chocolate brownies to cool completely then slice and serve.

AMERICAN FLUFFY PANCAKES

PREPARATION TIME
10 MINUTES

COOKING TIME
5 MINUTES

SERVINGS
4 PERSONS

INGREDIENTS:

- 90g plain flour
- ½ tbsp baking powder
- 2 tsp caster sugar
- ⅛ tsp fine salt
- 125ml milk
- 1 egg, lightly beaten
- 1 tbsp unsalted butter, melted
- 1 tsp spray oil
- 1 tbsp maple syrup

PREPARATIONS:

1. Preheat the Ninja Foodi to 175C for 5 minutes.
2. In a mixing bowl, whisk together the plain flour, baking powder, caster sugar and milk.
3. Then add the milk, egg and melted butter to form the pancake batter, allow the batter to rest for 5 minutes.
4. Spray the basket of the Ninja Foodi with oil then pour in the pancake batter.
5. Cook the pancakes for 5 minutes then remove the basket and tip out the pancake.
6. Slice the American fluffy pancake into four then drizzle with maple syrup and serve.

SESAME SEED PRETZEL BITES

PREPARATION TIME 20 MINUTES

COOKING TIME 5 MINUTES

SERVINGS 4 PERSONS

INGREDIENTS:

- 1 tsp fast action dried yeast
- 200ml water, room temperature
- 2 tsp caster sugar
- ½ tsp fine salt
- 175g plain flour
- ¼ tsp baking soda
- ½ tsp sea salt
- 2 tsp sesame seeds
- 2 tsp spray oil
- 2 tbsp unsalted butter, melted

PREPARATIONS:

1. In a bowl whisk together the yeast, water, caster sugar and salt.
2. Then gradually add the plain flour into the bowl, stirring to form a soft dough.
3. Cover the dough with a kitchen cloth and allow it to prove for 10 minutes.
4. Divide the dough into 8 then roll each into long strips and slice into bite-sized pieces.
5. Fill a saucepan with 1 litre of water and add the baking soda.
6. Bring the water to a boil then add the pretzel bites, cook for 15 seconds then remove for a slotted spoon.
7. Drain the bites onto kitchen paper then season each with sea salt and sesame seeds.
8. Set the Ninja Foodi to 200C and preheat for 5 minutes.
9. Spray the Ninja Foodi basket with spray oil then add the pretzel bites in a single layer.
10. Place the basket into the pot and cook for 5 minutes until crisp and browned.
11. Brush the sesame seed pretzel bites with melted butter then serve.

PEACH COBBLER

PREPARATION TIME 10 MINUTES

COOKING TIME 10 MINUTES

SERVINGS 4 PERSONS

INGREDIENTS:

- 500g canned peaches, drained
- 75g brown sugar
- 1 tsp cornflour
- 75ml water
- 120g plain flour
- 1 tsp baking powder
- ¼ tsp ground cinnamon
- 120g unsalted butter, diced

PREPARATIONS:

1. Place the canned peaches into the basket of the Ninja Foodi pot then sprinkle over the brown sugar.
2. Whisk together the cornflour and one tablespoon of water then pour the mixture into the pot.
3. Into a mixing bowl add the plain flour, baking powder and cinnamon, stir to combine.
4. Then add the diced butter, rub the butter into the flour using your fingertips to form a breadcrumb texture.
5. Spread the breadcrumb topping over the peaches then close the lid of the cooker.
6. Set the pot to COOK on high pressure for 10 minutes.
7. Allow for a quick release of pressure then serve the peach cobbler with vanilla ice cream.

BERRY OAT CRUMBLE TART

PREPARATION TIME
20 MINUTES

COOKING TIME
25 MINUTES

SERVINGS
6 PERSONS

INGREDIENTS:
- 150 g plain flour
- 120 g oats
- 120 g caster sugar
- ½ tsp baking powder
- 150 g butter
- 150 g blackberries, large ones halved
- 150 g blueberries
- 2 tbsp cornflour

PREPARATIONS:

1. Close the Ninja Foodi Pressure Cooker Air Fryer's lid and move the slider to the AIR FRY/STOVETOP. Preheat the pot by selecting BAKE/ROAST, setting the temperature to 325°F, and time to 5 minutes.
2. Select START/STOP to preheat.
3. Prepare the oat crumble by adding the flour, oats, caster sugar and baking powder into a mixing bowl. Combine and add the butter.
4. Once crumbly, spray the Ninja Multi-Purpose Pan with cooking spray add the crumble mixture. Press with your fingers to form a crust. Reserve half a cup of crumbs for the topping.
5. In a second mixing bowl, combine the blackberries, blueberries and cornflour and spoon over the crust. Top with the reserved crumbs.
6. Place the pan on the bottom layer of the Deluxe Reversible Rack in the lower position.
7. Close the lid and ensure the slider is still in the AIR FRY/STOVETOP.
8. Select BAKE/ROAST, set temperature to 325°F, and set time to 20 minutes.
9. Select START/STOP to begin cooking.
10. When cooking is complete, remove the rack with the pan and cool before serving.

BREAD AND BUTTER PUDDING

PREPARATION TIME 10 MINUTES

COOKING TIME 45 MINUTES

SERVINGS 4 PERSONS

INGREDIENTS:

- 4 slices white bread, diced
- 50g raisins
- 50g chocolate chips
- 2 eggs, lightly beaten
- 50g honey
- 200ml milk
- 1 tsp ground cinnamon
- 1 tsp vanilla extract
- 50g unsalted butter, melted

PREPARATIONS:

1. Place the diced bread, raisins and chocolate chips into the basket of the Ninja Foodi.
2. In a bowl whisk together the eggs, honey, milk, cinnamon, vanilla and butter.
3. Pour the mixture over the bread then stir to combine the ingredients.
4. Cover the pot with the lid and set to COOK at 170C for 45 minutes.
5. Release the pressure from the pot and serve the bread and butter pudding with fresh berries.

Conclusion

You have completed your first step to culinary freedom. You can now cook in an unheated kitchen.

The next step from here is to explore even further and find your own culinary footing! Learn the basics from this recipes, and come up with your very own awesome Ninja Foodi Friendly recipes and make your ultimate meal plan!

The Ninja Foodi possesses the unique ability to micro-wave food, so if you are looking for a one-stop-shop for your food-cooking needs, it really doesn't get any better than the Ninja Foodi! You see, with just one appliance, you will be able to make the staples of your diet! You will be able to make rice, soup, stews, pastas, deep fried foods, and vegetable dishes, all with the simple touch of a button! So, what you are telling yourself at. This is far too good to be true! I know, I know! Of course, the question on your mind would definitely be: how can the Ninja Foodi deliver such great attributes for such a low price? Instead of having to spend over a hundred dollars on a rice cooker, a slow cooker, and an air fryer, the Ninja Foodi has all of those functions in one tiny, inexpensive appliance. Not only does it have those attributes, but it is able to take your cooking to the next level. Now, you can make the most delicious steamed or deep fried foods in your own home! Your whole family will be motivated to eat clean and more often, all because you singlehandedly took control of your kitchen! Lastly, if you feel like your Ninja Foodi is just not up to snuff, don't worry! Ninja Foodi is not like any other appliance that you will probably ever encounter. A Ninja Foodist always trusts and follows their instincts, and you should too. The Ninja Foodist rewards us for doing so. Ninja Foodist that is what we ninja's are training to become. If you look at the Ninja Foodi Cam you'll notice that it is almost the same size as the Ninja Foodi itself, but for ninja training purposes we must use the Cam to train our reflexes. Just like one must when learning to use a silent but deadly weapon like the Shurikon. A Ninja Foodist learns to be able to respond to any situation in a relatively quick manner, and when training like this, we must do so much faster than ever before. Like Ninja Foodist's already do, we must do so while dealing with a situation on a much larger scale.

Fire is still a big deal, so keep on practicing … please. Try to avoid meat or fish in most of your meals, or you'll get massive heartburn. Enjoy your Ninja Cooking skills! It is fun to create new recipes and experiment. You don't need a microwave, just add foil, aluminum foil, etc to your dishes to be heated. Making beans in your Ninja Cooking is great. Since they are very water soluble, they will add their own water to your dish when you cook them. Plates, bowls, baking sheets and glass will work just as well as induction cooktops or a non-microwave oven.

You are now a culinary ninja. Enjoy cooking your favorite Ninja Foodi Friendly meals and recipes!

RECIPE INDEX

A
American fluffy pancakes	78

B
Bacon and potato hash	17
Baked potatoes	74
Beef Stew Dumplings	44
Beef and Root Veg Hotpot	45
Beef Stew with Dumplings	39
Berry Oat Crumble Tart	81
Bread and butter pudding	82
Breaded fish goujons	26
Buffalo cauliflower bites	63

C
Cheesy baked eggs	18
Cheesy Courgette Muffins	21
Chicken and Herb Bake	52
Chicken and mushroom	59
Chicken fajitas	57
Chicken satay	60
Chicken taco bowl	56
Chili verde	51
Chocolate Brownies	77
Chocolate mousse	75
Chunky Chips	13
Clam chowder	27
Corned beef and cabbage	42
Cottage Pie	14
Courgette fritti	73
Crispy French toast	19

E
Easy Fish Pie	33

F
Fish pie	30
Fried cabbage	70
Fried Halloumi	62
Fried shrimp	28

G
Garlic and Herbs Fish Pie	35

H
Herbed Salmon	23
Hotpot	43

K
Kedgeree	20

L
Lamb and Bean Hotpot	38
Leek and Potato Soup	66
Leek Rarebit Pork Steaks	47
Pork Sandwiches Slaw	46
Lentil soup	72
Loaded omelette	15

M
Mashed potato	64
Mustard Pork Steaks	48
Mushroom Risotto	65

O
Oatmeal	16

P
Peach cobbler	80
Potato salad	71
Prawn pasta	25

R
Raw Kale Tabbouleh with	62
Rice Pudding	76
Roast beef	40
Roasted root vegetables	68
Roast Lamb with Garlic	37
Roast Lamb with Ginger	36
Rocket Salad	61

S
Salmon Fishcakes	22
Sausage and onion gravy	41
Sesame seed pretzel bites	79
Shrimp alfredo	32
Shrimp boil	31
Sichuan peppercorn steak	50
Smoky Fish Gratin	34
Spatchcock chicken	58
Beef and Vegetable	43
Spring Roasted Chicken	53
Steamed broccoli	67
Sticky Chicken Wings	54
Stuffed Courgettes with	61
Sunday Roast Chicken	55
Sweet and Sour Pork	49

T
Tater Tots	69
Teriyaki salmon	24
Tuna casserole	29